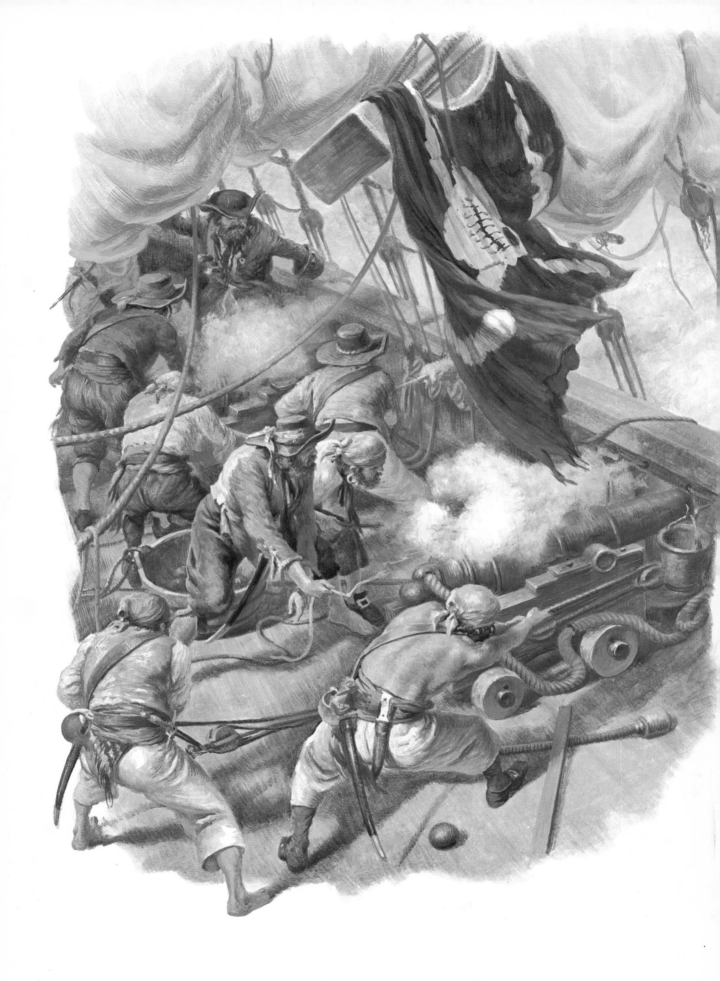

BUCCANEERS
and
PIRATES

by John Gilbert

Illustrated by
E. Mortelsman

HAMLYN

London . New York . Sydney . Toronto

Contents

Introduction

Chapter One p. 15

From the Barbary Coast to the Spanish Main

Chapter Two p. 41

Bravery and Brutality: the Pirates of Tortuga and Port Royal

Chapter Three p. 61

Adventure and misadventure in the South Seas

Chapter Four p. 73

French Corsairs of the Channel Coast

Chapter Five p. 89

The Pirates of Madagascar

Chapter Six p. 105

Piracy's Final Fling

Published 1975 by
The Hamlyn Publishing Group Limited
London . New York . Sydney . Toronto
Astronaut House, Feltham, Middlesex, England
© Copyright 1975 Éditions des Deux Coqs d'Or/Western Publishing
Company Inc.
ISBN 0 600 37093 3
Printed in France

INTRODUCTION

The black flag of piracy

On a fine spring day in 1717 a French merchantman carrying a rich cargo of wine, silks and ivory made a splendid sight. With white sails billowing in a fresh breeze, she ploughed a steady course westward through the calm waters of the Caribbean. The long voyage across the Atlantic had passed without incident, but after several weeks at sea the crew were impatient for their first glimpse of the West Indies.

The men were in cheerful mood. Soon there would be no more barked commands, monotonous shipboard chores, bouts of seasickness, dreary food and stale drinking water. Ahead were lazy, carefree, sun-drenched days and wild nights of drunken revelry.

The captain, however, with many transatlantic crossings to his credit and years of trading experience among the islands, knew that the indented coastlines of these beautiful Caribbean islands spelt danger. Any landlocked bay or creek might conceal a pirate ship, lying in ambush. Navigation through these shallow waters, with their treacherous rocks and reefs, demanded the utmost concentration and seafaring skill. A small pirate vessel, low in the water, had all the advantages of speed and manoeuvrability, and if more than one happened to be lurking, his bulky merchantman could be caught in an inescapable trap.

Trouble came sooner than he expected. Minutes after the lookout had joyfully yelled out his announcement of land on the port bow, the sails of a ship were sighted on the horizon. As the captain focused his telescope on the stranger, his worst fears were realized; for the black flag fluttering from the mainmast identified her unmistakably as a pirate ship. Inspection at closer quarters would have revealed the emblem on the flag as a skeleton in the guise of a devil, the hallmark of a pirate renowned for his bloodthirsty career of crime at sea – Edward Teach, better known as Blackbeard.

The French captain was confident that his forty cannon would be more than a match for this lightly-armed pirate sloop. Events soon proved him wrong. Blackbeard was no novice at this kind of fighting. Knowing that the higher-calibre French guns were only effective at long range, he steered his ship in close and opened fire, raking the French rigging with deadly accuracy. One well-aimed broadside, finding its mark, brought the enemy's main topsail crashing down in flames onto the deck, causing confusion and panic. Forced almost to a standstill, the larger vessel was now a sitting target, and within half an hour Blackbeard's men had swarmed triumphantly up the sides of their victim. The cargo was worth the taking, but even more welcome was the ship herself, which Blackbeard duly converted into his own flagship, renaming her the *Queen Anne's Revenge*.

Pirates all

Blackbeard was one of the most colourful and notorious pirates of all time, and his exciting story will be told in greater detail in the later pages of this book, the central characters of which are the daring, dangerous men (and even women) who sailed the high seas in the sixteenth, seventeenth and eighteenth centuries – the golden age of piracy.

Not all pirates, however, were as brutal and terrifying as Blackbeard.

The naval battle between the Egyptians and Philistines

The fact that they were described by various names – pirates, buccaneers, privateers, corsairs and so forth – underlines important differences between them. If they were captured, such distinctions could be issues of life and death.

The word 'pirate' comes from the Greek *peiratēs* and Latin *pirata*, meaning someone who attempts or attacks – hence a sea adventurer or robber. Such a man worked for himself, sailed his own ship, attacked the vessels of any nation, and kept everything he took from a beaten foe. In other places and at other times he would be called a freebooter, filibuster or buccaneer. 'Freebooter' came from the Dutch word *vrijbuiter*, meaning 'free booty'; the French rendered this as '*filibustier*', translated into English as 'filibuster'. The term 'buccaneer' was derived from the French word *boucan*, a wooden grill for smoking meat, and the original buccaneers were literally hunters of wild cattle. But whatever they called themselves, all these men were free-lance pirates.

A 'privateer' was a ship, or ship's captain, carrying official papers known as 'letters of marque'. These permitted the captain to attack enemy (but not neutral) shipping in time of war. But privateering expeditions were often organized in peacetime by governments or wealthy syndicates, who shared in the eventual profits. In a sense, therefore, it was piracy made legal. The word 'corsair', derived from the Latin *cursus*, meaning a race or course, is rather more confusing. It could refer both to a light, speedy type of sailing vessel and also to her crew. But the term came to have different meanings according to time and place. No comparison can be made, for example, between the fierce Barbary corsairs of the early sixteenth century and the high-principled French naval officers of the seventeenth and eighteenth centuries, who went by the same name. The former were ordinary pirates, the latter privateers supported by their government. Most of these privateers had good family backgrounds

9

(some were members of the nobility) and had received a wide-ranging education – valuable additions to seafaring and fighting experience. It was not by mere chance that privateering heroes such as John Hawkins and Francis Drake held high commands in the English fleet which shattered the Spanish Armada in 1588, that corsair captains such as Jean Bart, Claude de Forbin and René Duguay-Trouin led French warships into action against Britain and the Netherlands a century later; or that Jean and Pierre Lafitte helped the U.S. army to defeat the British at the battle of New Orleans in 1815.

The term 'piracy', as used in this book, covers the exploits of men of very different nations and backgrounds, united only by the fact that they lived, fought and often died in pursuit of adventure on the high seas.

'From the fury of the Northmen, O Lord, deliver us'

A long tradition

Bartholomew Roberts, last of the great pirate captains, met his death in 1722 on board his ship, dressed 'in a rich crimson damask waistcoat and breeches, a red feather in his hat, a gold chain around his neck, with a diamond cross hanging to it, a sword in his hand, and two pairs of pistols hanging at the end of a silk sling, flung over his shoulders.'* His crew could not have afforded such luxurious trappings, but certainly pirates throughout the ages prided themselves on looking the part. With their curling moustaches, red bandanas, eyepatches, gold rings on ears and fingers, and fearsome assortment of knives and pistols stuck into belts and sashes, they made sure they were recognized and respected. Their appearance in the cobbled streets and taverns of a sleepy fishing port must have had honest citizens behind their locked doors praying not to be caught up in an orgy of drunken rioting in which their money, their women and their lives might be at stake.

Piracy is an ancient profession. From the time nations first began trading with one another (about five thousand years ago) there were desperate adventurers who were prepared to risk their life and limb to win a valuable cargo of gold, copper, timber, spices or gems.

The Mediterranean, cradle of trade in the Western world, swarmed with pirates. In the twelfth century B.C., the Philistines or 'Peoples of the Sea' swept down from their hide-outs in the Aegean Sea, clashing with the fleet of the Egyptian Pharaoh Rameses III in the first naval battle ever recorded. The Egyptian bowmen caused panic by

*Charles Johnson, *A General History of the Robberies and Murders of the Most Notorious Pirates.*

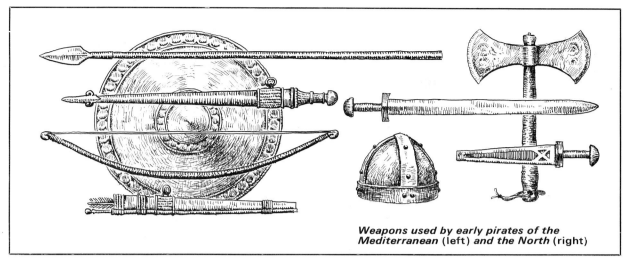

Weapons used by early pirates of the Mediterranean (left) and the North (right)

raining arrows down on the decks of the Philistine ships; then the soldiers clambered aboard, slaughtering the enemy seamen and tossing their bodies into the sea.

At about the same period the Phoenicians, bold explorers and colonizers, turned their hands to slave-trading and piracy. The Greek historian Herodotus describes how Phoenician raiders kidnapped the daughter of the King of Argos, and so sparked off the Trojan War. As for the noble Greek generals who, according to legend, sacked the city of Troy, the sulky Achilles and the cunning Odysseus were both self-confessed pirate chiefs; and another famous legend of Jason and the Argonauts, who sailed to Colchis in quest of the Golden Fleece (an adventure supposed to be partly based on fact) is really nothing more than a marvellous pirate story.

Caesar and the Aegean pirates

In 78 B.C., the young Julius Caesar had a dramatic brush with a gang of pirates from Asia Minor. The galley in which he was travelling was suddenly attacked and boarded by a terrifying mob of sword-brandishing ruffians. The quaking passengers cowered against the rails, but the young man in elegant clothes calmly continued reading. The pirate chief, seeing that he was educated and probably wealthy, offered to set him free for twenty talents, a very considerable sum. The arrogant youth looked contemptuously at the fierce bearded figure looming over him, then exclaimed, 'Twenty talents indeed! If you really knew your job you would realize that I was worth at least fifty!' Recovering quickly from his astonishment, the pirate leader accepted the higher offer on the spot, and took his captive to the Greek mainland, where he soon received the ransom.

Before long he was to regret this. Caesar, on his release, planned a fearful revenge. Marshalling four war galleys and packing them with five hundred troops, he attacked the pirates' headquarters, slaughtering most of the men while they were feasting and drinking. After recovering his ransom money, he bundled the survivors off to prison. Then he had them all executed by slow strangulation. 'I showed them mercy,' he commented later. 'I could have had them crucified!'

Vikings and monks

The seas surrounding the British Isles were rich hunting grounds for pirates. During the Roman occupation of Britain, a fleet commanded by Marcus

Aurelius Carausius was despatched, in A.D. 286, to deal with piracy off the coasts. But Carausius turned pirate himself, unleashing a reign of terror. In the end, his own legionaries arose in mutiny and murdered him.

After the Roman Empire crumbled, Vikings from Scandinavia swept down on Western Europe and the British Isles, raiding and plundering. 'From the fury of the Northmen, O Lord, deliver us,' chanted the monks of such remote islands as Lindisfarne, attacked by Viking marauders in A.D. 793. Fisher-folk and villagers along the exposed Atlantic shores anxiously awaited the next assault by the fierce warriors from the north, in their long, serpent-prowed ships.

Kings, princes and dukes often hired foreign mercenaries to do their dirty work. King John of England (1167-1216) employed a French exile known as Eustace the Monk, who had abandoned religion for the more profitable career of piracy. This 'master pirate' was reputed to be a magician as well, for several of his victims claimed that he could make his ship invisible!

'Serve me well,' said John, 'and I will reward you.' But Eustace looted enemy French towns and killed innocent people with so much zest that John, disgusted, proclaimed him an outlaw. Soon Eustace was back, full of contrition. John showered him with gifts and allowed him to build a palace. But after John's death, Eustace again offered his services to the highest bidder, this time to King Philip II of France, who invaded England in 1217. Eustace took command of the 'great ship of Bayonne', but the French fleet was defeated. When Eustace's ship was boarded, he was accused of treason and given the choice of being beheaded either on the bulkwark or astride the huge siege engine on deck. As one eye-witness dryly remarked, 'He had little desire for either, but they still cut it off.'

A dishonest penny

Throughout the Middle Ages, seemingly honest officials and merchants made

The buccaneers of Tortuga

fortunes out of smuggling and piracy. Two quaintly named brigands, Sterte-beker and Godekins, formed the 'Friends of God and Enemies of the World', a pirate group which plundered shipping in the North Sea and the Baltic. Stertebeker was finally captured and beheaded, with seventy of his men. Rumour had it that the mainmast of his ship was stuffed with an enormous quantity of gold.

In England many pirates ended their days dangling in chains at Execution Dock alongside the Thames. It was more difficult to punish the important men who hired and organized these ruffians. John Hawley, mayor of Dartmouth, personally captured thirty-four French merchantmen (considered fair game, since the two countries were at war) but added many Spanish and Genoese galleys to his score. Less fortunate was the Lord High Admiral, Thomas Seymour, brother of Henry VIII's third wife, who spent as much time organizing pirate expeditions as he devoted to official duties. Lord Seymour was arrested for high treason and in 1549 was beheaded on Tower Hill.

Thus on both sides of the Channel there were already many experienced seamen who, with the backing of greedy men with money, rank and power, were poised for any action that would result in profit. The discovery of the New World opened new gates to private and public wealth. Men's eyes now turned westward to the Spanish Main and the fabulous, mysterious land of gold – Eldorado.

Rules, romance and reality

A pirate crew might be a foul-mouthed, hard-drinking, quick-tempered lot, but they were subject to strict discipline.

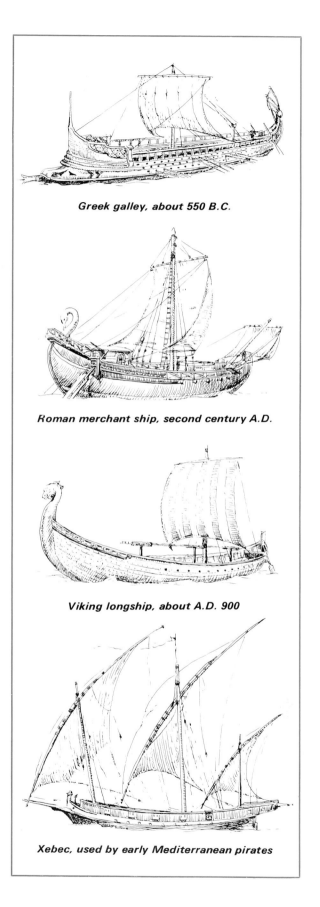

Greek galley, about 550 B.C.

Roman merchant ship, second century A.D.

Viking longship, about A.D. 900

Xebec, used by early Mediterranean pirates

13

The Pirates' Articles covered daily shipboard behaviour, treatment of prisoners and sharing of loot. There were 'insurance' schemes for injury in action and compensation to relatives in case of death. The Tortuga buccaneers received 600 silver pieces of eight* or six slaves (men captured from enemy ships) for the loss of a right arm; but an eye or a finger was worth only 100 pieces of eight or one slave.

For minor misbehaviour, such as being drunk, a pirate might be clapped in irons or flogged. For cowardice, disobedience or desertion he stood to be tried and shot. Personal feuds would often be settled by sword or pistol duel. Sometimes unruly pirates were marooned on a lonely island; despite the stories however, there is no evidence that any captain made a culprit walk the plank.

The basic condition for signing on was 'no purchase, no pay'. In other words, a pirate received no salary but could share in the spoils, in proportion to his rank, if and when a prize was taken. It was this lure of any easy fortune which united men from so many different social classes and backgrounds. The prospect of sighting a prize, crippling her with a broadside, clambering on board, slashing the enemy to ribbons in close combat, and sharing out valuable booty, was worth months of drudgery, boredom and discomfort. A successful pirate could win more in one day than an ordinary sailor could earn in an entire lifetime.

Most pirates 'made ends meet' by taking their share of plunder and then quickly squandering it on drink, cards and women. Some died of natural death, some perished of fever, starvation or exposure. Others died as violently as they had lived, felled by a cutlass stroke or musket shot, or dangling from the end of a rope. But there were a few who retired to a comfortable life. So long as a pirate could dream of fame and luxury, that was motive enough.

Here then are some of the most thrilling adventures of the pirates, filibusters, buccaneers, privateers and corsairs. For centuries they ruled the seas and changed the course of history.

*A silver coin, also called a peso or Spanish dollar, equivalent to eight reals and worth, very approximately, 30 pence.

Marooned

CHAPTER ONE

From the Barbary Coast to the Spanish Main

AT dawn on October 12, 1492 Christopher Columbus, followed by his officers, stepped from a longboat, splashed through the surf and planted the royal banner of Spain in the sand of a beautiful island in the Caribbean. The naked Indians who watched in amazement as he dropped to his knees, tears streaming down his cheeks, called their home Guanahani. Columbus renamed it San Salvador and claimed it for the Spanish Crown. After a three-months' voyage across the Atlantic, the Genoese sea-

man had not found an alternative route westward to the fabulous Spice Islands of the Orient. But although he did not know it, he had discovered what came to be known as the New World.

Columbus beckoned the natives to approach and handed them glass beads and trinkets to show that he came as a friend. Soon the Indians were rowing out in their dugout canoes across the bay where Columbus's three ships were anchored, bearing gifts of their own, including spears and brightly coloured

15

parrots. But what intrigued Columbus was the fact that some of them were wearing nose ornaments of pure gold.

Whatever the official motives for the expedition, Columbus was in no doubt that his main objective was gold. Using sign language, he questioned the Indians. Where did they get their ornaments from? Did they mine gold on this island and if so could they lead him to the spot? They laughed, shook their heads, chattered in their incomprehensible tongue and pointed out to sea. Columbus gathered that an enormous kingdom with unlimited supplies of gold lay somewhere to the south. Two days later he set sail again in search of a fortune.

It proved an elusive quest. He and his men explored more islands, entranced by their beauty. But although the natives were invariably friendly, when questioned about gold all they would do was to point vaguely over the horizon. Columbus was hopelessly confused as to his whereabouts, believing that he was off the coast of China and assuming that the land of gold must be Cipango (Japan). In fact, the first large island he reached was Cuba, and still his scouts failed to bring back any gold. Three weeks later he anchored off another island which he named España, known to other nations as Hispaniola. Here the rumours of gold were stronger, and one day an officer returned to camp in triumph, carrying a few genuine nuggets that he had exchanged with the local Indians. Much tempted to continue exploring, Columbus decided to sail home, leaving thirty-nine men behind with food and ammunition for a year – the first Spanish settlement in the islands which Columbus named the West Indies.

The world divided

King Ferdinand, Queen Isabella and their courtiers listened in rapt excitement as Christopher Columbus described his epic voyage, telling them of the beautiful islands and their handsome, dark-skinned inhabitants. Although their stay had been brief, the sights, sounds and scents of the lands they had explored still haunted their dreams. By day the sun blazed down on the golden sands, yet a cooling breeze always fanned the shore. The waters that lapped the beaches were incredibly blue and so crystal-clear that shoals of rainbow-hued fishes could easily be seen as they darted in and out of the rocks that studded the shallows.

Columbus' ships – Santa Maria, Pinta and Niña

Beyond the lines of palms fringing the sands were immense curtains of greenery – outposts of the dense tropical forests into which no men dared venture, for fear of poisonous snakes, giant spiders and terrible centipedes. From the treetops arose the screeching hubbub of countless exotic birds, invisible apart from an occasional dazzling flash of colour against the dark foliage as a parrot fluttered among the high branches. By night the moon would cast its silvery gleam on the gently rippling ocean and the air would be filled with the pungent perfume of tropical fruits and flowers.

This was a New World, whose natural treasures were surely beyond human imagination. As proof, Columbus showed the king and queen his gold nuggets, and he urged them to lose no time in sending him back to Hispaniola to look for other islands.

The prospect of gold and precious jewels spurred the Spanish monarchs to authorize Columbus to continue his explorations. In three later voyages he was to add new territories to Spain's overseas empire. But reports of his first expedition had already reached the court of Portugal. Portuguese navigators had reached the southern tip of Africa and were poised to forge a sea route westward to India. Spain wanted no interference in the newly discovered West Indies. So the rival nations divided the unknown world between them. Under the Treaty of Tordesillas, signed in 1494, an imaginary line was drawn in the Atlantic, from north to south. It was fixed about one thousand miles west of the Cape Verde Islands. All lands to the east of this line were to belong to Portugal (giving her a foothold in South America in 1500 when Pedro Álvares Cabral accidentally discovered Brazil), and all territory to the west of the line would go to Spain. This latter proved to be the lion's share, for it included the regions on the mainland of Central and South America which yielded the fabulous riches, notably gold and silver, of the Aztec and Inca empires. Columbus's successors, the sword-bearing, crucifix-carrying soldiers known as the Conquistadors,

The Barbarossas strike

received the credit for these discoveries, but it was the Caribbean islands, first found and settled by Columbus, which provided the bases for these expeditions of conquest.

The seafaring Protestant powers of Europe were infuriated at the cavalier fashion in which the two great Catholic nations had carved up the globe. France, England and the Netherlands also wanted a share in the gold of the New World. In the years to come they would give free rein to pirates and

privateers alike in the Caribbean, the area that came to be known as the Spanish Main. Strictly speaking, the Main comprised only the gold- and silver-producing countries of the American mainland, but the term was used to describe all the Spanish-held possessions in the West Indies as well.

The Barbary corsairs

In the early years of the sixteenth century, Spain faced a battle on two fronts. At first she was more concerned with events nearer home, where a serious threat was posed by the dreaded corsairs of the North African Barbary Coast.

The Barbary corsairs carried on the ancient traditions of Mediterranean piracy. Most of them were Moslems, nursing a bitter hatred of Catholic Spain and of Christianity at large. They preyed on European shipping and carried out lightning raids on ports and villages along the coasts of Spain, France and Italy. Moors and Christians clashed on land and at sea, and prisoners of both sides, if not executed, were often condemned to a lifetime of suffering as chained galley-slaves.

The galley had been the principal type of war vessel used in Mediterranean waters since the days of Ancient Greece and, astonishingly, it was still serving as a war vessel some 2,000 years later. With its beak-like projecting prow, it was basically a rowing vessel (although it also carried sails), with banks of oars either side, so heavy that each oar had to be handled by four or five men. The Barbary corsairs often preferred a lighter ship, also combining oars with sails, known as a galliot; and they sometimes dispensed with oars, using a three-masted sailing ship called a xebec. The latter was rigged both with square and lateen (triangular) sails. Square sails provided driving power, but lateen sails gave a ship greater manoeuvrability against the wind. The advantage of the speedy galliot over the broad, unwieldy galley was vividly demonstrated on a spring morning in 1504.

Arouj and Kheyr-ed-Din, the most famous of the early Moorish corsairs, were better known as the Barbarossa brothers because of their red beards. Cruising off the Italian coast on this pleasant sunny day, they quickly changed course when the silhouette of a huge war-galley appeared on the horizon. The galley was one of two such ships bound for Genoa, and they were owned by no less a person than the Pope himself. The captain, watching the galliot approaching at speed, had no suspicions, certain that pirates would never risk coming so close to land. But when the smaller vessel failed to alter course, and the gap between the ships narrowed to less than fifty yards, he sensed that something was wrong. Before he had time to alert his crew, a hail of arrows poured down on the deck of the galley, and he himself was wounded in the shoulder. Grimacing with pain, he remained conscious just long enough to see a horde of turbaned, battle-whooping Moors, their curved scimitars glinting in the sun, clambering on board. Some half dozen of the soldiers forming the galley's armed bodyguard kept their adversaries at bay with a deft display of swordsmanship, but many more dropped their weapons and dived overboard. It was only a matter of minutes before the pirates were in control and the corpses of Christians littered the deck. As the

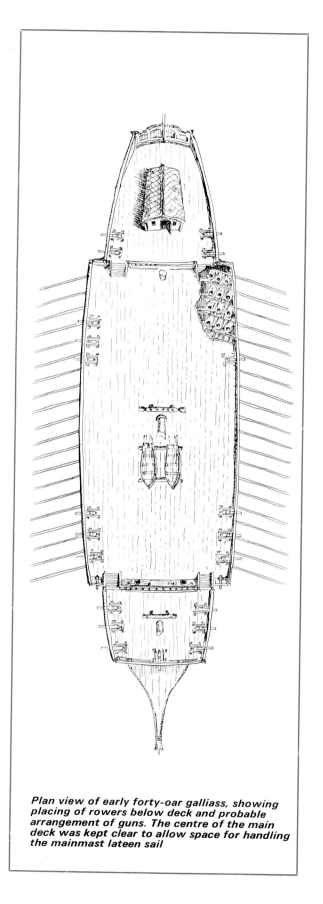

Plan view of early forty-oar galliass, showing placing of rowers below deck and probable arrangement of guns. The centre of the main deck was kept clear to allow space for handling the mainmast lateen sail

stunned survivors were herded below, the elder of the Barbarossa brothers, commanding the corsair vessel, stroked his bushy red beard in satisfaction.

In the late afternoon the second Christian galley hove in sight, and the Barbarossas planned a cunning trick to capture her. Arouj ordered his Moorish crew to strip the prisoners and to transform themselves into peaceful European seamen. The captain of the second galley saw nothing amiss. Suddenly a tall, red-bearded figure detached himself from a working group and barked an order to his disguised bowmen to open fire. For the second time that day the enemy was taken by surprise as the Barbary corsairs swarmed aboard to hack down the helpless Christians at close quarters. Finally Barbarossa gave orders for all the Moslem galley slaves to be freed and their places taken by the Christians.

The one-armed assassin

Some years later, the Spaniards bombarded the corsair bases in North Africa, and Arouj lost an arm in battle. Vowing revenge, he made a pact with the Algerians and helped them to drive the Spanish occupation forces from the Barbary Coast. But his real ambition was to rule Algiers unaided and unchallenged, even if this meant double-crossing his allies.

One day Barbarossa paid a visit to the Emir's palace. He was a familiar figure at court, and on this occasion was not even accompanied by bodyguards. Calling out a friendly greeting to the soldiers on duty at the gates, he marched confidently into the palace and was directed to the shady courtyard where the Emir was bathing in a pool. Putting on a secretive air, Arouj suggested that the servants be dismissed. When the two men were alone, Barbarossa stooped as if to whisper a message, grasped the Emir by the throat with his single hand, hauled him out of the water and strangled him by the side of the pool. Leaving the body slumped on the ground, he then calmly walked out of the palace, cheerfully saluting the guards as he went. He was confident that there was now no prince in North Africa powerful enough to prevent him from becoming supreme ruler of Algiers.

His success, however, was short-lived. Having rebelled against Spanish tyranny, Arouj could only retain power by treating his own enemies and critics with the same brand of savage cruelty. So many innocent people were tortured and executed on his orders that the time came when Spain and Algeria joined forces to overthrow him. Abandoned by his troops, Barbarossa fled from Algiers on horseback into the desert, trying to shake off his pursuers by strewing the sand with his treasures. Finally he was cornered like a wild animal in a rocky ravine and slashed to death by enemy swordsmen. They left his bleeding body for the vultures.

The heiress of Fondi

Arouj was succeeded by his younger brother Kheyr-ed-Din, equally brave and far more intelligent, who restored the corsair fortunes by forming an alliance with the arch-enemy of Christendom, the Sultan of Turkey. The last Spanish garrison in North Africa, on the offshore island of Peñon, was reduced to rubble after two weeks of cannon bombardment and the vanquished commander was publicly flogged to death. Barbarossa's corsair fleet terrorized peaceful shipping in the Mediterranean and sailed through the Straits

of Gibraltar into the Atlantic to ambush Spanish merchants on the final home stretch of their long voyage from the New World.

In the course of one well-planned terror raid against the Italian mainland, Kheyr-ed-Din decided to show his gratitude to his patron, Sultan Suleiman the Magnificent, by offering him a present. The unusual gift he chose was a beautiful, aristocratic lady from the town of Fondi, named Julia Gonzago. The only problem was that since the lady was married she would have to be kidnapped. Saddling his horse, Barbarossa galloped off into the gloom of the Italian countryside. Shortly after midnight he reached the sleeping town of

Kheyr-ed-Din leaves the burning town of Fondi

The battle of Lepanto

Fondi and started battering at the door of the Gonzago mansion. Unfortunately for him, somebody had warned the lady of his plans, and she had ridden away on horseback with a servant a few hours beforehand. Kheyr-ed-Din was so furious at his failure that he ordered the town to be burned to the ground and the entire innocent population slaughtered.

Fate never caught up with the younger Barbarossa, and he continued to destroy shipping for many years. He bought himself a pretty young Italian wife and eventually retired, wealthy and notorious, to Constantinople, where he died, of old age, in 1546.

Bluff and double bluff

Apart from the unfortunate Fondi episode, Kheyr-ed-Din had served Suleiman well and had helped the Turks to win naval supremacy in the Mediterranean against the fleets of Venice and

Spain. The Sultan found another willing ally in the successor of the Barbarossas, a former galley-slave named Dragut whose hatred of the Christians knew no bounds.

Dragut had been near to death when, by a stroke of luck, he was recognized, straining at the oars of a Venetian galley, by an officer who had himself been a galley-slave of the younger Barbarossa. This officer had persuaded the famous Genoese admiral, Andrea Doria, to ransom Dragut. It proved to be a rash decision, for the pirate chief had retaliated by embarking on a campaign of destruction in the true Barbarossa style. By a stroke of irony, Admiral Doria was in command of the Christian fleet dedicated to drive the corsairs from the Mediterranean. The enmity of the two men had all the bitterness of a personal vendetta.

There was one occasion when Doria must have felt that victory was in his grasp. In 1550 his ships carried out a surprise attack on the island base off the North African coast where Dragut was careening (cleaning and repairing) his ships. Dragut's vessels were temporarily immobilized on the shores of the island's inland lake, which was connected by a narrow channel with the sea. Since this waterway was well protected by Dragut's guns, Doria decided that his best policy was simply to blockade the entrance and starve the pirates out.

After several weeks of inactivity, Doria elected to brave the enemy guns and storm the lake. As his ships sailed down the channel he was relieved, yet somewhat puzzled, to note that the guns were unmanned. The reason became clear as he sailed into the lake. The corsair fleet had escaped. Dragut

Careening a pirate vessel

had calmly enlisted a local work force to dig a new channel from the opposite end of the lake, and had towed his ships out by night!

Dragut did not survive to witness Andrea Doria's crowning revenge against Turkey and her corsair allies twenty years later, in 1571. In the last pitched naval battle fought by oar-propelled ships, off Lepanto in Greece, Admiral Doria's galleys formed part of the Christian fleet under Don John of Austria. The Turks were routed and the dominance of the Barbary corsairs ended.

Gold on the high seas

Fifty years before the battle of Lepanto, Spain stood poised to claim what was hers by right of conquest – the huge empire in the New World which Columbus had promised but never lived to see. On a December morning in 1522, Hernando Cortés, self-proclaimed ruler of the Aztec empire, watched three caravels set sail from the Mexican port of Vera Cruz. They carried gold coins and ornaments, exquisite jewels and magnificent feathered head-dresses and cloaks – spoils from the palace of the

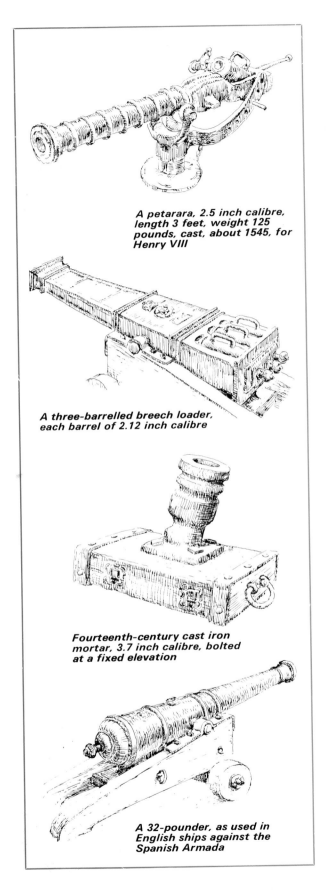

A petarara, 2.5 inch calibre, length 3 feet, weight 125 pounds, cast, about 1545, for Henry VIII

A three-barrelled breech loader, each barrel of 2.12 inch calibre

Fourteenth-century cast iron mortar, 3.7 inch calibre, bolted at a fixed elevation

A 32-pounder, as used in English ships against the Spanish Armada

former Aztec king Montezuma, who had surrendered eighteen months previously. The 45,000 gold pesos on board represented the royal 'fifth' and were tangible proof of the vast potential wealth of Spain's new possessions. Unfortunately the precious cargo never reached its destination.

In 1521 war had broken out between Spain and France, and French privateers were already taking a heavy toll of enemy shipping in the Atlantic. Jean d'Ango, a shipowner of Dieppe, was reaping handsome profits from these sea battles. One of his boldest and most trusted captains, Jean Fleury, was cruising off the Azores as Cortés's caravels ploughed steadily eastwards on the last stage of their voyage to Cadiz. Several larger armed caravels had joined them to convoy the treasure home.

From the distance Fleury could not be sure of the identity of the ships he planned to attack. Were they Portuguese or Spanish? It did not greatly matter. If bound from the Caribbean they would be Spanish, and their cargoes of hides, sugar or timber would be a welcome addition to the long string of successes already chalked up by his privateering fleet. He decided to concentrate his fire on the armed escorts and chuckled to himself as he saw them turn tail after letting off only a few token, ill-aimed rounds. His ships closed in on the remaining three unprotected caravels and soon forced them to surrender. When his men boarded the ships; they found, to their amazement, every available corner piled high with coins, jewels and priceless ornaments. During the hand-to-hand fighting, Cortés's second-in-command, Alonso de Avila, was captured, but far more rewarding was the unexpected treasure which soon flowed into the coffers of the French King Francis I.

The Spaniards later gained partial revenge by capturing the celebrated corsair. Before he was beheaded, he boasted that he had taken or sunk upwards of 150 Spanish ships, including galleons. This was an impressive haul, even bearing in mind that the term 'galleon' was at that time used to describe a variety of three- or four-masted sailing ships. It included both the caravel (which weighed sixty or seventy tons) and the carrack, midway in size between the caravel and the massive galleons of over five hundred tons that were later turned out from Italian, English and Spanish shipyards in the middle years of the sixteenth century. Used both for commerce and war, the later galleons were built with broader hulls to carry the weight of the additional guns that ran the entire length of the ship between decks. This made the ships rather unwieldy, and the elaborately carved and ornamented fore and stern castles merely added to the top-heavy effect, proving more of a hindrance than a help when speed and manoeuvrability were all-important. Sometimes the galleons were crammed so tightly with treasure or packed with so many passengers that they could not be filled with the normal quota of cannon. This is one reason why, on so many occasions, they gave such a poor account of themselves in battle and were routed by smaller vessels.

During the twenty or thirty years after Fleury's first victory against the Spanish treasure ships, French pirates and privateers repeatedly ambushed the vessels carrying gold from Mexico and silver from Peru. Jean d'Ango himself captured nine silver ships in the

Fleury's men reap their reward

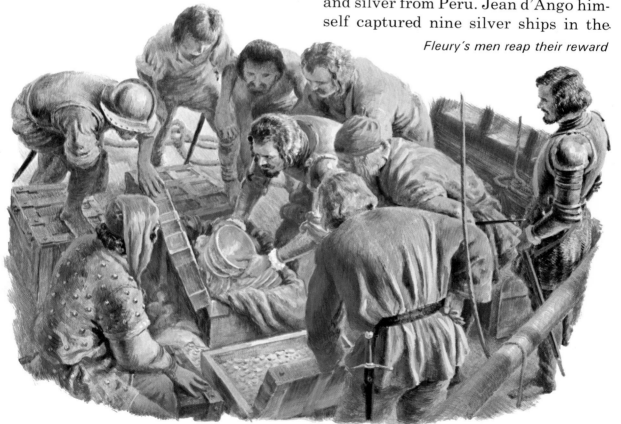

Bahama Channel. Although a large proportion of the treasure fleets got through safely, the Spanish authorities soon devised a proper convoy system. By mid-century, armed galleons were providing support for the two fleets which travelled to and fro across the Atlantic every year.

The nightmare of Havana

In 1555 the Cuban port of Havana was a settlement rather than a town, but it was vitally important as a centre of Spanish trade and communications in the Caribbean. It was here that two treasure fleets made their rendezvous, laden with the riches of the New World. The first fleet, known as the *galeones*, came from Portobello on the isthmus of Panama. Here the ships took on the heavy gold bars and silver ingots brought up by mule train from the Peruvian mines and then carried across the isthmus by the *Camino Real* (Royal Road). The second fleet, the *flota*, sailed

from Vera Cruz with Mexican gold, silver and other merchandise. Laden with ingots, plate, emeralds and pearls, cochineal and ginger, hides and dye-woods, cocoa and sugar, they made a brief halt in Havana before embarking on the hazardous four-thousand mile voyage home.

When war between Spain and France flared up again in 1552, the Caribbean islands were obvious targets for attack. For those fortunate few who survived, the eighteen-day occupation of Havana by the French in July 1555 was a nightmare. The townsfolk were well aware of the possibility of being attacked, for a powerful French fleet of privateers commanded by François le Clerc, more familiarly known to friend and foe as Jambe-le-Bois (Wooden Leg), had raided settlements on the coasts of Puerto Rico and Hispaniola; and only the previous year word had reached

26

them that his second-in-command, Jacques de Sores, had ransacked Santiago de Cuba. Both men, and most of the crew members, were Huguenots, whose patriotic fervour was inflamed by religious hatred for all Catholics. De Sores was the more fanatical of the two, and it was Havana's fate to be at his mercy when he captured the port. Wealthy citizens were stripped of their treasures, then slaughtered; priests were insulted and brutally tortured, churches looted and desecrated. No prisoners were taken, for killing was the order of the day. When there was hardly a silver coin or gold ornament that had not gone to fill his holds, de Sores burned Havana to the ground.

Although the Spaniards took counter-reprisals they were unable to defend every square mile of their possessions; and soon they had a new enemy – with the growing naval might of England.

John Hawkins, slave-trading privateer

John Hawkins, commander of the battered seven hundred-ton *Jesus of Lubeck*, owned by Queen Elizabeth I, faced a terrible dilemma one September day of 1569 as he sheltered from the storm that had driven him to a point only a quarter of a mile from the Spanish-held Mexican coast. The little port of San Juan de Ulua was hardly more than a bank of rock and shingle, and it was a mere fifteen miles from the port and garrison of Vera Cruz; but for the time being it provided refuge for his three ships.

This was his third voyage to the West Indies, all of which had brought him honour and profit from the sale of African slaves, a commodity which the Spaniards were always ready to buy,

even from their hated rivals and enemies, the English. But Hawkins had already had more than enough excitement this time. The rickety *Jesus* had all but capsized in Atlantic gales before even reaching Africa; and once there, the Portuguese had given him an unexpectedly hostile reception, as had

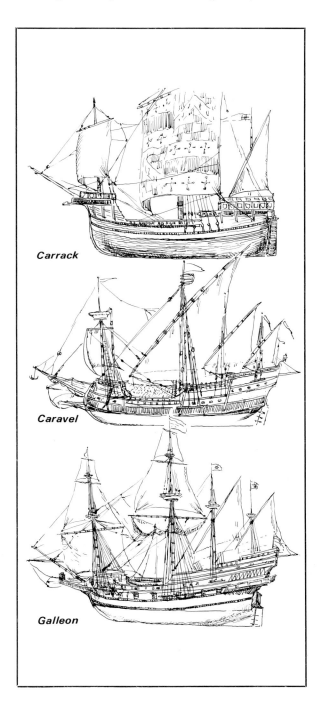

Carrack

Caravel

Galleon

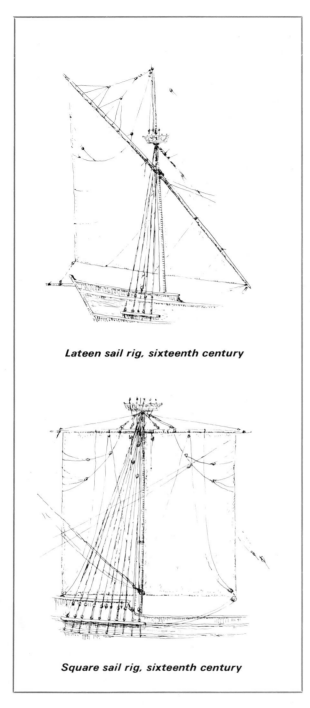

Lateen sail rig, sixteenth century

Square sail rig, sixteenth century

Hawkins had sold his slaves and was impatient to get home before the hurricane season struck, but the storms hit him as he rounded the western tip of Cuba. The *Jesus* in particular was badly damaged and since (in his own words), '. . . she was the Queen Majesty's ship and . . . should not perish under his hand', he made for San Juan de Ulua. Here, surprisingly, the Spanish authorities permitted him entry, under the impression that his vessels formed part of the *flota* which was expected daily.

Hawkins knew that the treasure fleet was due and lost no time in taking possession of the islet and the guns covering the harbour. He was just in time, for the following morning his look-outs reported the approach of the plate fleet – eleven merchantmen, escorted by two war galleons. On board the flagship, as Hawkins soon found out, was Don Martin Enriquez, newly appointed Viceroy of New Spain. It was the appearance of the Spanish fleet that placed Hawkins in a quandary.

The Queen had instructed him not to interfere with Spanish shipping and a pitched battle was in any case the last thing he wanted. Apart from the badly leaking *Jesus*, he had only the three hundred-ton *Minion* and the tiny fifty-ton *Judith*. The commander of the *Judith* was his cousin, Francis Drake, but the lad was young and inexperienced. Quite clearly the English were outnumbered and outgunned. On the other hand, if he tried to bar the *flota* entry to a Spanish port, possibly exposing the ships to the fury of hurricanes, even worse trouble might arise.

After three days of chilly but polite negotiations, Hawkins agreed to allow the Spanish ships to anchor alongside his own. A bargain was struck with the

some of the local chieftains. He had been compelled to join forces with the King of Sierra Leone, besieging and burning down a fortified town which had yielded several hundred prisoners. He still felt a pang of conscience when he recalled how the other survivors had been butchered and eaten by his victorious allies.

Viceroy. The English would be permitted to buy food and water and would be given time to repair their ships. Both sides agreed not to resort to violence and to exchange hostages as signs of good faith. But in truth Don Martin had no intention of keeping his word, seeing no reason to make a deal with a bunch of common pirates. Even while hostages were being exchanged, the Viceroy completed his plans for attacking the English ships and recapturing the island's guns. For this purpose he reinforced his fleet with soldiers from the garrison at Vera Cruz, slipping them on board his merchantmen under cover of darkness.

The battle of San Juan de Ulua

Hawkins rightly suspected treachery but was strangely unprepared for the surprise attack which was launched two days after the Spaniards anchored. Hawkins's gunner on the *Jesus*, Job Hartop, who later wrote an account of the episode, described how his captain was just sitting down for a meal when one of the Spanish hostages drew a knife from his sleeve and made a threatening lunge at Hawkins. The man was immediately disarmed, and after making sure he was locked up, Hawkins rushed on deck with a crossbow.

The naval battle at San Juan de Ulua

The first stage in the Spanish attack was already in progress. One merchant-man was seen closing in on the *Minion*, and on her deck was the Spanish Vice-Admiral, Juan de Ubilla. Hawkins shouted across that he was hardly behaving like a gentleman. 'I am doing my duty as a fighting man,' Ubilla yelled back. Hawkins's reply was to loose a warning arrow at him, but it flew wide. Ubilla then signalled his flagship, the trumpets on the Spanish vessels blared across the water.

The soldiers concealed on the enemy ships poured out and soon overpowered the English shore party, recapturing the guns. Only three sailors escaped, swimming out to the *Jesus*. Hawkins was alert enough to repel a group of enemy soldiers trying to board the *Minion*, and all three English ships kept up a steady stream of fire, sinking four Spanish vessels. One burst of

Job Hartop sentenced to the galleys

grapeshot exploded the powder maga-zine of the Spanish flagship and she went down, but the water was so shal-low that she was not put out of action.

Soon the tide of battle turned. The enemy cannon on shore shot away the masts of the *Jesus* and Hawkins him-self had a narrow escape when, accord-ing to Hartop, he called for a cup of beer, which was smashed by cannon shot the moment he put it down. 'Fear nothing,' remarked the unruffled cap-tain, 'for God who has preserved me from this shot will also deliver us from these villains!'

Brave words, however, were not enough to win the day. Hawkins even-tually abandoned the *Jesus*, transfer-ring men, supplies and treasure to the *Minion*. Night now brought a halt to the fighting, and the two surviving ships removed themselves out of range of the shore batteries. The next morn-ing was stormy and the *Minion* was almost wrecked. Worse still, the *Judith* had vanished. As Hawkins wrote later, 'With the *Minion* only and the *Judith* we escaped, which bark the same night forsook us in our great misery.' No explanation for Drake's apparent de-sertion was ever given, and Hawkins never alluded to the incident again.

The *Minion's* return voyage was a nightmare. The ship was hopelessly overcrowded, and half the crew were put ashore at a deserted spot on the Mexican coast, preferring to risk cap-ture by the Spaniards or Indians rather than face the terrors of the Atlantic. Some of these died of starvation, some were killed, others were imprisoned in Mexico. The more unfortunate of the survivors were later tried by the Spanish Inquisition and tortured, flog-ged or sent to the galleys. The gunner

Job Hartop was to spend twenty-three years in Spanish prisons or galleys.

As for those who chanced their luck with Hawkins, only fifteen out of one hundred were alive when, after three months, the *Minion* anchored at Mount's Bay in Cornwall. The men had been forced to eat vermin and stewed hides when the food ran out. Drake, in the *Judith*, had been luckier, bringing most of his crew home and arriving in Plymouth five days before his cousin.

For the famous privateer who had won his country such wealth and renown in former years, the voyage was an almost total disaster. He had lost ships, men and treasure. He would not return to the Caribbean for more than twenty-five years, and then only to meet his death.

Francis Drake: master thief of the unknown world

Francis Drake, who had not forgotten the English humiliation at San Juan de Ulua and his own sorry showing in the battle, soon made amends. Within five years, his fame resounded through the Spanish Main. The Spaniards disdainfully called him a pirate, a master thief, a sea-dragon, yet grudgingly paid him respect for his daring and honourable behaviour. This stocky, grey-eyed, ruddy-faced man, with his neat pointed beard, commanded the affection and loyalty of his men, and to the people of England he was a great hero. In the pages of history, Drake is the very symbol of the romantic, adventurous, swashbuckling Elizabethan age.

Drake felt instinctively that his destiny lay in the West Indies. In the summer of 1572, he launched a daring attack on the terminus of the Peruvian gold and silver convoys, the port of Nombre de Dios (popularly called the 'treasure house of the world'), on the isthmus of Panama. Landing with seventy-four men in a sandy bay outside the town, Drake caught the enemy by surprise. Armed with muskets, cross-bows and firepikes*, the invading party entered Nombre de Dios in two groups from opposite ends of the town. One group was led by Drake himself, the other by his lieutenant, John Oxenham, assisted by Drake's brother John. There was little enemy resistance, but during one brief skirmish an English sailor was shot dead and Drake was struck in the leg by a stray musket shot. In the excitement of directing the attack, he was unaware of the pain. Within a few minutes he met Oxenham's party, which had advanced without challenge. As they gazed at the empty square and deserted streets, it gradually dawned on the English that Nombre de Dios was at their mercy.

Drake wounded at Nombre de Dios

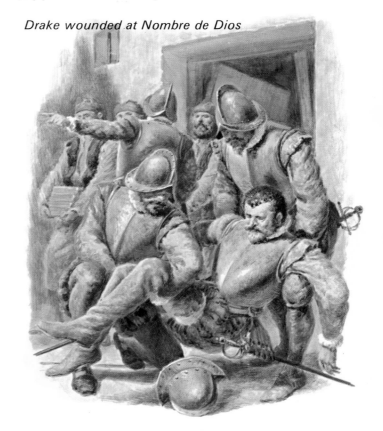

The few prisoners that had been taken were forced to lead the raiders to a house near the square where hundreds of silver bars were piled high to the roof of the cellar, but to the amazement of his men, Drake abruptly ordered them not to touch anything. The real prize, gold, was locked in a treasure house close to the beach. It was essential to act quickly. Already the streets were swarming with frightened citizens, and the Spanish soldiers who had fled, thinking that the invading force was much larger, were surely planning a counter-attack. Oxenham and John Drake began battering down the doors of the warehouse. Suddenly Francis Drake collapsed, blood oozing freely from his injured leg. 'Leave me here,' he begged. 'Take as much gold as you can, then get back to the boats – but hurry!' Oxenham made the only possible decision. Despite Drake's protests, he was carried down to the beach and lifted into a pinnace. Then the whole group rowed out, empty-handed and dejected, to the ships lying at anchor. The treasure of Nombre de Dios remained intact. But the time would come, and fairly soon, for Drake to turn failure into glorious success, and to gain a fortune beyond his wildest dreams.

Ambush in the forest

Infuriated by the mishap at Nombre de Dios, Drake decided to set an ambush for the Spanish mule convoy itself, as it wound its way slowly across the isthmus with gold and silver for the *flota*. In 1573 he enlisted the help of some African slaves known as Cimarrons (or Maroons), who had escaped from their Spanish masters and now lived in the mountains of Panama, overlooking the Royal Road. After four weary days of trekking through the jungle, weighted down by their heavy armour and weapons, Drake's men reached a ridge. The leader of the Maroons mo-

Drake ambushes the treasure convoy

tioned Drake and Oxenham to clamber up to a rough platform built across the fork of a tree. In amazement, the two Englishmen saw behind them the familiar waters of the Caribbean, but ahead was another great expanse of blue sea. For a few moments neither of them spoke. They knew they were looking down on the Pacific, that immense South Sea charted by Magellan. Deeply moved, Drake prayed that God should spare him to be the first Englishman to sail a ship on that ocean; and beside him John Oxenham vowed to follow his captain. The dreams of both men were to be fulfilled, Drake's ending in triumph, Oxenham's in tragedy.

When they reached an ideal spot for their ambush, Drake ordered his men to crouch in the undergrowth. It seemed an eternity as they lay there, sweat pouring from their bodies, insects nipping at their exposed hands and faces. No breeze ruffled the broad canopy of leaves overhead. Now and then a man

let out a muttered oath or a nervous laugh. The stifling heat, the uncanny silence and the bodily discomfort of hours of waiting built up an atmosphere of almost unbearable tension. Suddenly jingling bells were heard in the distance. It was the mule train. As the sounds grew louder, each man stiffened and held his breath. But at the last moment there was a fatal mishap.

One of the men, obviously drunk, jumped from his hiding place. A couple of Maroons pulled him back into the bushes and the incident was over so quickly that Drake did not even notice it. But the damage had been done, for the man had been spotted by the leader of the convoy, who galloped back down the track to warn his companions. Drake, not suspecting anything was wrong, remained in hiding. The tinkling bells could now be heard clearly, and as he peered through the foliage he dimly made out the shapes of animals. There were fewer mules than he had

'Where is the silver?'

expected, and he let them come within twenty yards before giving the signal to attack. There was no resistance from the muleteers and no shooting. The reason was soon plain. The pack-saddles contained provisions and nothing more. The rest of the convoy had been pulled off the track. Somewhere in the gloom of the forest armed soldiers were waiting for Drake's next move. Rightly suspecting a trap, Drake angrily withdrew his band. Once more he had been cheated of his treasure.

Undeterred, Drake joined forces with a French privateer named Têtu and planned a second attack, promising to share the spoils evenly. The English pirates who had taken part in the previous ambush were sullen and reluctant, but even they brightened up when the five Maroon scouts reported the approach of a large convoy of one hundred and ninety mules, every one carrying gold or silver. This time Drake

kept his men on a tight rein – no whispering, no moving and certainly no drinking. As the leading mules plodded slowly along the narrow forest path, the pirates sprang out from either side. Although there were only thirty-four of them, the few dozen escorting soldiers apparently thought there were more. After letting off several random shots, one of which hit Têtu in the stomach, they galloped off for reinforcements, leaving the muleteers undefended. This time the pirates found, to their joy, that there was more gold and silver than could possibly be carried back to base. They stuffed their pockets and waistbands with the gold, but Drake made them bury the silver, intending to return when the coast was clear. Then, as the sound of echoing hooves gave warning of the imminent approach of fresh enemy horsemen, each man drifted off into the forest.

Soon the Spaniards were in hot pursuit. One drunken Frenchman, weighted down with gold, was captured. He was forced to reveal where the silver was buried and was then executed. The Spaniards soon dug it up but failed to overtake the other pirates and their gold. The unfortunate Têtu, however, faint from loss of blood, was found lying beside the path. He was beheaded on the spot.

Despite the loss of the silver, the gold that Drake shared out when he reached the coast was enough to justify the raid. Added to this was a vast quantity of treasure which Drake had amassed by plundering Spanish forts and ships along the Panama coast, while awaiting his chance to ambush the mule convoys. No previous pirate or privateer had ever won such a fortune. During the fourteen months that he had

34

been in the Caribbean, Drake had captured and burned more than a hundred Spanish ships, fought off superior numbers of highly trained enemy troops with only a few dozen men, and spread terror up and down the coasts of the Spanish Main. More significantly, he had collected a fortune in gold, silver and jewels; he sailed home not only famous but wealthy too. From now on he was Spain's deadliest enemy.

The ordeal of John Oxenham

In 1576, three years after he had peered down at the Pacific, John Oxenham robbed Drake of the credit for being the first English commander to take a ship into those waters. With the aid of friendly Maroons, he paddled down river in a pinnace to the shores of the South Sea and captured two treasure-laden barks bound from Peru. But the adventure ended tragically, for he made the mistake of freeing the crews, who soon put Spanish troops on his trail.

As he camped with his men in a forest glade, Oxenham little suspected that the Spaniards had already discovered his pinnace and the treasure hidden in nearby thickets, and that they now surrounded his party. But although the small band fought bravely, they were overwhelmed and Oxenham lost eleven men. He and the survivors were taken in chains to Panama City. There, according to an eye-witness, he was asked 'whether he had the Queen's licence or the licence of any other prince or lord for his attempt. And he answered he had none, whereupon he and all his company were condemned to die, and so were all executed saving the captain, the master, the pilot, and five boys which were carried to Lima; there the captain was executed with the other two.' The boys were spared.

Drake captures the 'Spitfire'

There was great excitement on the Sunday afternoon of March 1, 1579, on board the *Golden Hind*, commanded by Francis Drake. Hero of the hour was the captain's cousin, young John Drake. He had won the golden chain which

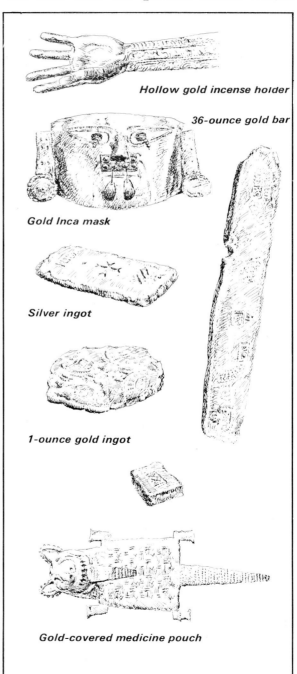

Hollow gold incense holder

36-ounce gold bar

Gold Inca mask

Silver ingot

1-ounce gold ingot

Gold-covered medicine pouch

had been promised to the man who first sighted the treasure ship *Nuestra Señora de la Concepcion*, popularly known as the *Cacafuego* ('Spitfire'). The *Cacafuego* was the pride of the Spanish navy, a huge galleon, currently bound from Peru to Panama with a fortune in silver. Drake knew that this was probably the most valuable prize ever encountered during his eventful career at sea. The *Golden Hind* was making good speed just off the coast of Ecuador, and Drake reckoned that the Spanish vessel on the horizon was about nine nautical miles away*. He was in no hurry. It would be safer to launch a surprise attack under cover of darkness. So, in order to cut down the speed of his ship, he gave orders for a string of water-filled wine jars to be towed from the stern.

It was fifteen months since Drake had sailed from the English port of Ply-

Francis Drake and San Juan de Anton

mouth on a voyage which was to make history. His flagship had then been called the *Pelican*, a sturdy one hundred-ton three-master, carrying eighteen demi-culverins (cannon firing a nine-pound shot). Four smaller ships had sailed proudly in his wake on that winter morning. Now he was alone, separated from the rest of his fleet after battling the gales in the Straits of Magellan. It had been a heart-warming moment, six months previously, when he had finally rounded the tip of South America and entered the Peaceful Sea that had haunted his dreams ever since that tantalizing glimpse of blue from the tree platform in Panama. In celebration of that dramatic day when he had turned north for the first time during the voyage, Drake renamed his ship the *Golden Hind*, from the crest of one of his chief patrons, Sir Christopher Hatton.

Drake was not sure of the expedition's official aim. One set of orders told him to search for the elusive southern continent which map-makers called *Terra Australis Incognita*; another set instructed him to explore trading possibilities with the Portuguese in the Spice Islands. But Drake knew very well what he and his backers (including Her Majesty) wanted more than anything else – Spanish treasure.

So far he had met with disappointments and little success. One surprise raid on the Peruvian port of Callao, where a few Spanish ships lay at anchor, had yielded a small quantity of gold plate, silks and linen. Yet the psychological impact of the raid had been tremendous. This was a secure Spanish stronghold and the authorities were thrown into panic by the fact that there was an English ship in the Pacific,

*A nautical mile or sea mile is equivalent to about $1\frac{1}{6}$ ordinary miles.

and that ship commanded by the master pirate himself, Drake the dragon.

Drake's careful plans for attacking the *Cacafuego* were really unnecessary. Despite her size, the galleon was lightly armed and her captain, San Juan de Anton, having received no prior warning from Callao, was confident that the *Golden Hind* was friendly, probably carrying a message for him. So he changed course, and by nine o'clock that evening the two ships were within hailing distance of each other.

'Who are you?' bellowed the Spaniard.

'A ship from Chile,' was the reply.

San Juan brought his ship alongside when, to his alarm and amazement, he heard English voices shouting, 'We are English! Do you understand? English! Strike sail or we send you to the bottom!'

Angrily the Spanish captain retorted, 'What kind of old tub is this telling me to strike sail? Come aboard and do it yourselves!'

Drake took him at his word. The whistle for action on the *Golden Hind* was defiantly answered by a trumpet blast from the *Cacafuego*. Drake's men rained arquebus shots and arrows onto the deck of the galleon, and a single round of cannon fire tore down her mizzen mast, toppling it, fully rigged, into the sea. As armed English sailors, brandishing bows and guns, swarmed over the side, the Spanish crew fled, leaving San Juan alone on the deck.

Staunchly refusing to tell them where the captain and pilot were, San Juan, for the moment unrecognised, was bundled on board the *Golden Hind*, there to be politely greeted by Drake, who was just pulling off his helmet and removing his armour. 'Be patient,' he told his defeated enemy, 'for this is what happens in war!' Then he locked him in the poop cabin under strong guard.

When the *Cacafuego* was searched, it was found to be carrying a fortune exceeding Drake's wildest expectations – thirteen chests of pieces of eight, eighty pounds of gold bars, twenty-six *tons* of silver (one Spanish sailor watching it being transferred to the *Golden Hind* suggested the galleon be renamed *Cacaplata*, or 'Spitsilver', and an unspecified quantity of plate, pearls and other jewels). In terms of plunder it was more than enough to pay for the whole expedition and to make Drake one of the wealthiest men in England.

Drake's men also discovered sea charts outlining the route followed by the galleons plying from the newly settled Spanish port of Manila in the Philippines to Acapulco in Mexico, a piece of top-secret information. Drake hoped to crown his success by intercepting the Manila galleon with its silks, satins, muslins, spices and perfumes from China and the Orient, but it was not to be. Reaching a point on the American coast just north of modern San Francisco (a cove which he named Drake's Bay) and claiming the surrounding territory of New Albion for the Queen, Drake sailed across the Pacific to the Spice Islands. There he took on six tons of cloves (half of which had to be heaved overboard with eight demi-culverins when the *Golden Hind* hit a reef in the Malay Archipelago). Finally he brought his ship home via the Cape, anchoring in Plymouth after an epic round-the-world voyage.

Despite strong protests from the Spanish ambassador, Queen Elizabeth conferred a knighthood on Drake. He had brought home treasure worth (in modern values) more than £10,000,000. Out of the eighty men who sailed with him, fifty-nine survived – a good proportion in those days when fever took such a large toll at sea.

Last word for the lady

Piracy had its risks, but in Queen Elizabeth's day, as in any other age, justice was not always impartial. The important things were who you were or whom you knew. A case in point was the celebrated Killigrew affair.

Sir John Killigrew was a high-ranking government official, whose family wealth came from the proceeds of a smuggling and pirating syndicate. The

Top secret – the Manila galleon route

Killigrews owned ships, financed illegal ventures, bribed port and customs officials, and had an underground network of agents who disposed of the goods. Sir John's handsome mansion overlooked the harbour of Falmouth, and one of the most indefatigable members of the family was his elderly mother, who sometimes played a more than passive part in the proceedings. One winter day in 1582, Lady Killigrew received information from her spies that a Spanish ship had been driven by storms into the harbour below, and that there was a cargo of silver on board. Bad weather prevented the ship from leaving Falmouth, so, on a particularly dark, rough night when the Spanish officers were drinking ashore, the old lady led a boatload of armed ruffians in an attack on the ship. The skeleton crew put up a brief, confused resistance but in a few minutes they were lying dead on the deck. Lady Killigrew's men ransacked the ship and returned with their booty, undetected, to the family mansion.

Unfortunately, the Spanish owners of the looted ship reported the raid to London. After an enquiry, Lady Killigrew was arrested and tried. Since piracy was a capital offence (the two nations not being at war), the court sentenced her, as ring-leader, to be executed. But at the last moment the Queen granted a reprieve. Two of Lady Killigrew's servants went to the scaffold in her place!

The defeat of the Armada

When war finally broke out between England and Spain in 1585, it was Sir Francis Drake and his privateer companions who were given command of the ships that crushed the invading

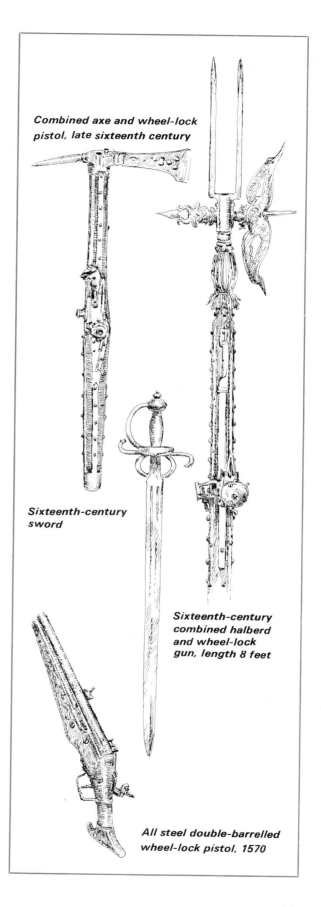

Combined axe and wheel-lock pistol, late sixteenth century

Sixteenth-century sword

Sixteenth-century combined halberd and wheel-lock gun, length 8 feet

All steel double-barrelled wheel-lock pistol, 1570

Armada three years later. As a prelude, in 1587, Drake had boldly sailed into Cadiz harbour and 'singed the King of Spain's beard', destroying many of the ships massed for the invasion of England. Now he commanded the *Revenge*.

Even in the heat of this, the first great pitched battle between sailing ships, Drake's privateering instincts did not desert him. Slipping away on his own (an action for which he was severely reprimanded) his path crossed the crippled Spanish galleon *Nuestra Señora del Rosario*. Her captain immediately surrendered and Drake took more than 200 soldiers prisoner, landing them on the Dorset coast. As a bonus, he helped himself to the 55,000 ducats on board.

The newly designed Spanish galleons carried heavy guns, some capable of firing a fifty-pound shot. But the culverins on the English warships, although they fired only a fifteen- or twenty-pound shot, could be swivelled and had a longer range. After three indecisive engagements, the English panicked the Spaniards by launching fireships downwind into the middle of their fleet. Then they battered the enemy ships at point-blank range. Forced by storms to retreat northward, the remnants of Philip II's proud Armada struggled home, around the tip of Scotland and down the Irish coast, where many were wrecked. Of the 130 ships fifty-one failed to return. The English did not lose a single ship. It had been a crippling blow to Spanish supremacy.

Last sight of the Caribbean

Seven years after the crushing of the Armada, Drake and Hawkins sailed for the last time to the West Indies. The venture was badly planned and the two heroes could not agree on a common plan of attack. On the evening of November 12, 1595, before a raid on San Juan de Puerto Rico, Sir John Hawkins died in the cabin of his flagship. Drake sailed on, dreaming of conquering Panama. But as his ship lay at anchor off Puerto Bello, he was struck low with dysentery. On the night of January 27, 1596, Sir Francis Drake died. The following day his grieving men lowered his coffin into the calm blue waters of the Caribbean.

CHAPTER TWO

Bravery and brutality: the pirates of Tortuga and Port Royal

Hardly a ripple stirred the placid, deep blue waters off the north coast of Cuba on a May day in 1628. As Admiral Pieter Hein surveyed his thirty-one powerful warships strung out in a broad arc so as to block entry to the Florida Straits, he was in confident mood. His scouts had done their work well. The sails of the leading galleons of the Spanish fleet from Mexico were already visible on the horizon, and the steady course they were steering made it clear that they had no suspicion of the trap that

lay ahead. Experienced seaman though he was, Piet Hein's heart raced a little faster as he watched the line of galleons looming larger every minute. There seemed to be a wide gap between the nine leading ships and the four bringing up the rear of the convoy. So much the better, thought Hein. If, as he assumed, the latter were the guard vessels, they would be too late to rescue the nine merchantmen that were now almost within range of his guns. At last, after years of raiding in the Carib-

41

The Dutch board the foundering galleons

making up the Lesser Antilles. Here they were already planning to grow tobacco and other agricultural crops. The Dutch, soon to be followed by England and France, had set up a West India Company to organize trade and to finance the new island settlements. The southern tip of the island chain pointed towards Trinidad and the exposed shores of the weakly defended Spanish Main; the northernmost islands looked westwards to the Spanish outpost of Puerto Rico, two hundred miles away. Beyond that lay Hispaniola, Jamaica and Cuba, commanding the treasure routes. And it was here that Admiral Piet Hein had set his ambush.

The trapping of the treasure fleet

The Spanish galleons, judging by the erratic course that they now began steering, had finally spotted and identified the Dutch warships, but their plight was hopeless. Piet Hein's fleet was closing in from three sides: within half an hour the circle was complete, the trap sprung. The nine merchantmen were cut off from their escort vessels, too far away to lend any assistance. Only a few warning salvoes across the bows of the nearest ships were needed before the flags of surrender were raised. Piet Hein was delighted that his tactics had succeeded. But as he turned his attention to the four larger galleons which were now lying almost motionless a safe distance from the action, he realized he might still have a battle on his hands. Individually each of the Spanish vessels was more strongly armed than his, but in terms of combined strength (seven hundred cannon and three thousand men) the Dutch had a tremendous advantage. However

bean, the greatest prize of all, the treasure fleet, lay within his grasp.

It was now forty years since the Spanish Armada had been defeated, and the situation in the West Indies had meanwhile been completely transformed. Spanish ships no longer dominated the seas and Spain's island empire was crumbling. The Dutch republic, struggling for independence against Spain, now had a strong navy and her ships were spreading terror throughout the Spanish Main. The way was already clear for English, French and Dutch settlers, reinforced by privateers and pirates, to take possession of the unoccupied 750-mile-long chain of islands

bravely they resisted – and Hein had no great opinion of Spanish fighting morale or ability – there could be only one outcome.

Piet Hein was right. The four escorting galleons were so overloaded with cargo and extra passengers that the crews were unable to man the guns in time. As the Dutch warships bore down, they turned and fled in the only direction possible, toward the Cuban coast. Predictably, the lumbering ships ran aground. With the Dutch guns trained on them at point-blank range, they offered no resistance as longboats were lowered and armed sailors clambered aboard.

The booty, most of it carried in the escort vessels, was colossal. In addition to hides, cochineal, indigo, dyewoods, cocoa, sugar, ginger and spices, the Dutch sailed home with pearls, gold and silver worth about fifteen million guilders – a fortune. It was a great personal triumph for Piet Hein, an unbelievably profitable enterprise for the Dutch West India Company, and yet another blow to Spanish prestige.

Pierre le Grand: first Tortuga buccaneer

In 1635, some seven years after Piet Hein's famous victory, another enemy of Spain was cruising in the Caribbean, off the west coast of Hispaniola. But Pierre le Grand, born in Dieppe, was no admiral with a fleet of warships and thousands of fighting men. His vessel was a frail, leaking sloop, and the twenty-eight buccaneers who made up his crew were dirty, desperate and weak from lack of food and water. Their captain, unshaven, his face deeply tanned from long exposure to the tropical sun, was dressed in the same tattered clothes

as his men, and was doing his best to revive their drooping spirits. Weeks ago they had sailed from their island base of Tortuga, confident of waylaying a Spanish merchantman. But luck had been against them. In familiar waters, bearings could always be taken from prominent landmarks, but once out of sight of the coast, accurate navigation was difficult, sometimes impossible. There were no sea charts of this area and le Grand's compass and cross-staff were of little use, now that the rudder was damaged beyond repair. After endless days of tacking aimlessly to and fro, the sloop was drifting helplessly with wind and current, the crew grateful still to be alive.

The Spanish colony on Hispaniola was no longer prospering. In the west

First of le Grand's victims – a sentry

Lateen-rigged dugout outrigger, favoured by pirates of the Caribbean, and based on the dugout design used by the Fiji islanders. The larger dugouts of this type were often armed with a cannon or swivel gun.

ous – *boucaniers*, or buccaneers.

At first they roamed the hills and valleys, trading hides, dried meat and tallow with the crews of passing ships, in exchange for clothing, tobacco, brandy, guns and ammunition. In time some of them were strong enough to take over the small, rocky, thickly forested island of Tortuga, two miles north-east of Hispaniola. Tortuga, so named because it was shaped roughly like a turtle, grew into one of the most important buccaneer bases in the Caribbean.

The settlers of Tortuga, initially French and English, continued to hunt and to buy meat from Hispaniola, but soon many of them took to the sea for a livelihood, sailing out in canoes and lateen-rigged dugouts. These were the *filibustiers*, or freebooters. But whatever they called themselves, their main occupation was piracy. Around the time that Pierre le Grand was active, the Spaniards launched an attack and almost wiped out the entire settlement, but the survivors gradually straggled back, once more posing a permanent threat to Spanish shipping and to the Spanish Main.

Pierre le Grand was apparently very different from the typical buccaneer who was only interested in drinking and gambling. No ordinary ruffian, he was level-headed, intelligent and extremely courageous. But even his spirits were beginning to wane as his sloop continued to drift, with no land in sight. It was doubtful if she could remain afloat for much longer.

The crew had almost abandoned hope when one evening the sails of a ship were sighted on the horizon, red in the setting sun. Le Grand soon identified it as a Spanish galleon, probably separ-

of the island, early attempts at farming and planting had been abandoned, and the land was fast reverting to scrub, overrun by wild pigs and cattle. It was now the haunt of corsairs, castaways, deserters and criminals. Most of them were French but there were also renegades from Flanders and Holland – all united in their bitter hatred of the Spaniards. Here they lived as hunters, cooking and curing their beef and pork in the native Carib Indian style by laying the strips of meat over a slow fire. The Indians called this process *barbecu*, the French *boucan*; and it was from this method of smoking meat that the hunters of Hispaniola acquired the name by which they were to become notori-

ated from the main body of the treasure fleet. Despite murmured protests, le Grand urged his men to prepare for an attack. 'True,' he admitted, 'she is stronger than we are. But what can we lose? If we go on as we are, we shall all be dead in a few days anyway. Lie low until it gets dark and we'll give them a surprise!'

A surprise attack

It was pitch black when the buccaneers paddled in close enough to the treasure ship to make a boarding attempt. As they gazed up, the twinkling stars were completely obscured by the immense hull and high rigging of the galleon. Creaking and rocking, she towered above the tiny pirate ship like a giant menacing a dwarf. By now the sloop was close to capsizing. To emphasize that there was no alternative, le Grand ordered his men to bore holes in the stern and sink her. Then the buccaneers slowly pulled themselves, step by step, up the swaying side of the galleon. Clutching desperately to any footholds they could find, until they were able to attach grappling hooks and ropes, they finally reached the deck. For a few minutes they lay motionless, utterly exhausted by their effort. Fortunately, they had not been heard either by the steersman or by the single sentry on deck. Both were felled with pistol butts, then bound and gagged. Le Grand and a few companions, their pistols and cutlasses in hand, tiptoed toward the lighted poop cabin, where they could clearly see the Spanish captain playing cards with his officers. Meanwhile, the main party of pirates was sent to deal with the remainder of the crew below decks.

The four card-playing Spaniards leapt to their feet, thunderstruck with amazement, as le Grand kicked open the cabin door and levelled a pistol at their heads. 'Surrender at once, with your ship,' he barked. There was a long pause as the immaculately uniformed officers stared, petrified, at the filthy, ragged creatures that had suddenly appeared out of the night. As the two groups stood confronting each other,

An interrupted card game

the silence was abruptly shattered by a burst of firing from below. The attack on the crew's quarters had obviously met some resistance. As the captain and his men took advantage of the momentary disturbance to dash for the door, le Grand and his men opened fire and shot them dead. Silence outside suggested that the other buccaneers had completed their mission too. Le Grand ordered all prisoners to be locked up and the dead flung overboard. When his men searched the galleon, they found chests crammed with gold and other precious merchandise – the very fortune they had despaired of ever winning.

The plunder was divided, le Grand as captain taking the largest portion. At that point he made an unusual but very prudent decision. 'I propose sailing home to Dieppe with our prize, he announced. 'Those who do not want to come with me will be landed at Port Royal in Jamaica.'

Thanks to his daring and bravery, le Grand was now a rich man. His pirating days were over and, so far as is known, he ended his days in contented retirement.

Montbars the Exterminator

From his schooldays, the young Montbars had nursed one ambition – to fight and kill the hated Spaniards. His uncle was a privateer and when war broke out he included the lad among his crew bound for the Caribbean. The chance to prove himself came when the French frigate was attacked by a galleon. Montbars refused to stay below and threw himself into the hand-to-hand combat with such fury that his shipmates muttered unbelievingly that the boy looked like an 'angel of extermination'. The name remained with him ever after. In his late teens he was already leading punitive expeditions against the Spaniards on Hispaniola and freeing their Indian slaves. A man of massive build, with tanned skin and enormous bristling eyebrows, he was known simply as Montbars the Exterminator.

Montbars himself was a temperate man, drinking only water and refusing

Montbars's first taste of battle

to gamble. His men, however, were a motley crew – ferocious with their untrimmed beards and moustaches, dressed in ragged shirts, leather jackets and leggings stained with animal or human blood, moccasins of stiffened pigskin on their feet. Some of them carried long-barrelled French muskets, with a powder pouch and bullet bag, others had hatchets and knives dangling from their belts. Sometimes they would vary their attire with jackets, jerseys, boots and tricorn hats taken from dead and wounded Spaniards, together with pistols and swords to swell their armoury.

Most of our information about the appearance and lives of the early buccaneers, as well as the colourful des-

criptions of their exploits, came from the pen of Alexander Oliver Exquemelin, probably a Dutchman. Exquemelin was once an indentured servant (a slave on a plantation), picked up enough medical knowledge to call himself a surgeon, and eventually joined the buccaneers. His book *The Buccaneers of America* was first published in Dutch and later translated into several languages. Each version of the book was altered in subtle ways to glorify the exploits of its own nationals, and it was not surprising that the Spanish translation was particularly scathing towards men such as Henry Morgan, their archenemy.

Exquemelin began his book with vivid descriptions of the plants and animals of Hispaniola – some of which were based on pure imagination – and then went on to tell how the early buccaneers lived. The men who called themselves the 'Brothers of the Coast' were certainly a rough, violent, hard-drinking lot, yet it seems that they had to obey a number of rules that were common aboard pirate ships everywhere – sharing plunder, claiming compensation for injury and treating their prisoners mercifully. It is hard to believe that buccaneers such as Montbars stuck too closely to these rules. Apparently when he captured a Spanish ship he would slaughter the crew without a vestige of pity; and he was said to have invented some unpleasant forms of torture that set the pattern for later pirate leaders, such as ripping out the intestines of his enemies! But Montbars is a mystery man and there is so little information about his later adventures that some of these lurid accounts may owe more to legend than to fact.

Rock Brasiliano: master of bluff

Another remorseless early buccaneer, probably born in Holland, was Roche or Rock Brasiliano, so named because, until 1641, he had his headquarters on the coast of Brazil, where Dutch seamen and colonists had gained a foothold against the Portuguese. His contempt for the Spaniards was so intense that, according to Exquemelin, he roasted some prisoners alive on a wooden spit.

Brasiliano won fame by capturing a Spanish silver galleon and went on to terrorize merchant shipping. His men would often land at some peaceful fishing port, they would rampage, blind drunk, through the cobbled alleys, letting off pistols at any unfortunate passers-by who failed to get out of their way fast enough, and helping themselves to whatever took their fancy – a roll of cloth, a piece of jewellery or a pretty girl. Port Royal, one of Brasiliano's haunts and a town seething with every form of vice, had no liking for his drunken, brawling crew. They put up with the buccaneers so long as they had cash to spend, but breathed sighs of relief when they sailed off on another adventure.

By this time hit-and-run assaults on the poorly defended settlements of the Spanish Main were commonplace. In one attack on the town of Campeche in Mexico, Brasiliano was carrying out a reconnoitre in a canoe, with ten of his men, when he was captured by the enemy. He was locked in a prison cell and sentenced to be hanged. Although aware that there was little chance of escape, he wrote a letter and managed to get it delivered to the governor of the town, who was deceived into believing that it came from another band of buccaneers advancing on Campeche. It informed him that strong reinforcements were on the way and that terrible vengeance would be taken on the garrison if Brasiliano and his companions were harmed. The petrified governor lost no time in setting his prisoners free, in return for a promise that they would give up piracy! Needless to say, Brasiliano and his exultant crew were soon back at sea, plundering Spanish ships and settlements with more enthusiasm than ever; and neither the governor of Campeche nor of any other town

Priming a matchlock musket. The musketeer is pouring priming powder into the pan which he then closes. He pours a measure of powder into the barrel and follows with the shot, using the rammer beneath the barrel. He clips the slow match into the serpentine; the musket is ready. 1. Powder flask. 2. Priming pan. 3. Charger. 4. Slow match. 5. Serpentine.

Bartholomew the Portuguese reaches safety

on the Spanish Main got a second chance to put an end to this cunning, brutal buccaneer.

Overboard to safety

Perhaps recollecting this error of judgement, when the Spaniards again captured a pirate captain off the coast of Cuba, they decided to take no chances. The name of this Jamaica-based buccaneer was Bartolomeo el Portugues (Bartholomew the Portuguese). Instead of imprisoning him on land, they flung him into the hold of a ship in Campeche harbour and built a makeshift gallows on deck so that he could be hanged the next morning.

Bartholomew, who spoke fluent Spanish, overheard some sailors jubilantly discussing his fate and made up his mind not to give his enemies that pleasure. Foolishly, they had left him in the charge of a single sentry. The night was black and all was quiet as the buccaneer chief slipped up behind the unsuspecting soldier and slit his throat.

Success depended, of course, on his being able to slip overboard silently and somehow reach the shore. Since he was not a strong swimmer, Bartholomew made himself a pair of simple water-wings out of two empty earthenware wine-jars, stoppered with cork. Lowering himself gently over the side, he managed to keep himself afloat as he paddled unnoticed to the mainland.

For three days he lay hidden in the forest, while patrols of Spanish soldiers hunted for him. When the coast was clear, he set off along the shore away from Campeche, avoiding the main road, feeding on sea snails and berries. To ford river estuaries he fashioned a rough raft out of pieces of driftwood, lashed together with creepers. After two weeks of weary travel, he sighted a ship at anchor. Fortunately for him, it was manned by buccaneers from Port Royal. Thirsting for revenge, Bartholomew persuaded them to sail him back to Campeche. Then at dead of night he and his new shipmates boarded the very vessel from which he had escaped, killed the crew and sailed away to Jamaica.

Bartholomew the Portuguese was one pirate, however, who found out that crime does not always pay. In spite of many daring exploits he died in poverty, a bitter, forgotten man.

The bloodstained hands of L'Olonnois

In Exquemelin's book there is a picture of a fashionably dressed young man with long hair, a contemptuous look on his handsome face, a raised cutlass in his hand. He stands there, coldly challenging, against a lurid background of flames, billowing smoke, sinking ships, drowning men and corpses on the sand. This is how an unknown artist imagined the Frenchman Jean François Nau, better known as L'Olonnois, after the village in Brittany, Les Sables d'Olonne, where he was born in 1630. Exquemelin was obviously fascinated by this villain, devoting three chapters to his exploits. Even allowing for the fact that the author was mainly concerned to write a colourful, swashbuckling narrative, and often let his imagination rove freely, L'Olonnois emerges as the most notorious and bloodthirsty of the later generation of Tortuga buccaneers.

In the thirty years since the first Spanish massacre of the Tortuga settlement, the island's fortunes had changed. By 1640 an ex-naval captain named Le Vasseur had driven out the English. Later he turned it into a fortified stronghold, from which filibusters and buc-

L'Olonnois terrorizes Maracaibo

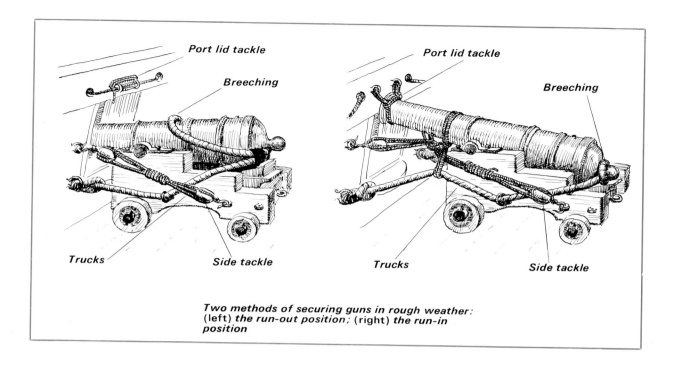

Port lid tackle

Breeching

Trucks

Side tackle

Port lid tackle

Breeching

Trucks

Side tackle

Two methods of securing guns in rough weather:
(left) *the run-out position;* **(right)** *the run-in*
position

caneers sailed out to raid the Spanish Main. At one point it was offered for outright sale to England for £6,000, but in 1665 it was a thriving colony administered by the wealthy *Compagnie des Isles d'Amérique*, with a French governor. In her efforts to become the leading naval power in the West Indies (a claim that could only be disputed by England) France found the seagoing experience of the buccaneers of Tortuga and Petit Goave, on the west coast of Hispaniola, most useful. Recognizing ambition and talent, the governor granted L'Olonnois a letter of marque, authorizing him to prey on Spanish shipping. L'Olonnois well repaid his patron's confidence, treating his prisoners with unspeakable cruelty, slaughter in cold blood being the most merciful of his methods.

Yet L'Olonnois had courage as well as natural cunning. Once when wrecked off Campeche, the Spaniards cut down his exhausted companions as they staggered up the beach. L'Olon-

nois smeared himself with blood and lay spreadeagled in the sand, pretending to be dead. When it was dark, he headed for the woods, stumbling now and then over the body of a slaughtered companion, until he reached the outskirts of Campeche. For several hours that night he wandered in disguise through the narrow streets of the Spanish port, and escaped in a canoe at the very moment when his enemies were celebrating his death with bells and bonfires!

L'Olonnois went from strength to strength, and in 1667, now in command of a small private fleet, he attacked the port of Maracaibo, at the entrance to Lake Maracaibo, on the Gulf of Venezuela. This town, regularly sacked by pirates, must have been one of the least desirable settlements on the Spanish Main. Having overrun the fort guarding the town, the buccaneers went to work on those unfortunate residents who had not prudently fled to the

The fate of L'Olonnois

surrounding hills with their valuables. L'Olonnois personally hacked one prisoner to pieces with his cutlass when the man refused to reveal where the town's treasures had been hidden. When torture failed to yield any useful information, the pirates went on a two-week looting and drinking spree, and then attacked the small settlement of Gibraltar at the opposite end of the lake. Routing the much stronger Spanish garrison, they held the town for a month, demanding 10,000 pieces of eight as ransom money. Then they sailed back to Maracaibo and extorted twice that amount. Herding together eight hundred and fifty head of cattle, they finally took their leave, 'causing great joy to the inhabitants . . . to see themselves rid of this sort of people'.*

In a later raid on Puerto Cavallo, in Venezuela, the buccaneers meted out death and destruction and avoided a

*Exquemelin.

Spanish ambush in the forest outside the town, forcing their prisoners to guide them to safety. Exquemelin describes (and the incident is dramatically illustrated) how L'Olonnois, beside himself with fury and impatience, ripped the heart out of one of his living captives and 'began biting and gnawing it with his teeth, like a ravenous wolf, saying to the rest, "I will do the same to you all if you do not show me the right path."'

In 1671 our 'hero' met a suitably grisly end himself. Abandoned by his comrades in the Gulf of Honduras, he and a handful of loyal followers fell into the clutches of a tribe of savage Carib Indians. Whether or not they knew who he was or what he had done, the Caribs ' . . . tore him in pieces alive, throwing his body limb by limb into the fire and his ashes into the air.' If the story is true – and one cannot imagine that any witnesses were left alive to tell the tale – no more fitting style of death could have been devised.

Henry Morgan raids Portobello

In 1668, the Spanish town of Portobello, on the east coast of the isthmus of Panama, was a hot, unhealthy, fever-ridden place, with some 3,000 inhabitants. But because of its importance as a trading centre, it was strongly garrisoned and its harbour dominated by a number of forts. It was off this coast that Sir Francis Drake had died. Now, some seventy years later, another English seaman lurked off the Spanish Main, having embarked on a career of piracy which, in the opinion of his countrymen, revived memories of the great Elizabethan hero. His name was Henry Morgan.

The island of Jamaica had been captured from Spain by an English fleet in 1655, and the seedy town of Port Royal soon rivalled Tortuga and Petit Goave as a base for buccaneers and privateers. Young Henry Morgan, who was born in Wales in 1635, was the son of a farmer and had taken to the sea during his Caribbean under the Dutch buccaneer Edward Mansvelt. When Mansvelt mysteriously disappeared, after a raid on Nicaragua, Morgan was elected to succeed him and assembled a powerful fleet of his own; and in the summer of 1668 he sailed, with the governor of Jamaica's blessing, from Costa Rica with nine ships and 460 men. The target of attack was Portobello.

On paper it looked suicidal. Morgan was well aware that he was outnumbered by three or four to one; but he silenced the more faint-hearted members of his crew by advancing the somewhat shaky argument that the fewer the numbers the more plunder there would be for every man who managed to survive!

Morgan was experienced enough not to risk a frontal attack on the heavily defended town. Choosing a point about thirty miles down the coast, a small flotilla of canoes and rowing boats paddled silently through the night, clinging to the shore. Skeleton crews were left on board the larger vessels, so that the fleet could sweep triumphantly into the harbour of Portobello the next day. In the small hours of the morning, the assault parties beached their boats and began wading through the swamps towards the town, now only a few miles distant.

The first objective was a fort on the outskirts of Portobello. Since it was the farthest from the sea and apparently in no danger of attack, the Spanish sentries, bored with routine on this hot, sticky night, were in relaxed mood. As one of them gazed sleepily across the empty expanse of swamp, he was suddenly seized by unseen hands. A knife poised at his throat and a gag of wood over his mouth prevented him from crying out. Without raising the alarm, the small English party bound their

Through the swamps to Puerto Bello

Ladders for the final assault

prisoner and hustled him back to be questioned by Morgan. After telling all he knew about the disposition and strength of the town's defences, the terrified Spaniard was frog-marched back in the dim light of dawn, with Morgan's buccaneers close on his heels. Fanning out in a semi-circle, they rushed the fort and scaled the walls before the unsuspecting soldiers knew what was happening. Once aroused, however, the Spaniards offered stout resistance and there was a brisk exchange of musket fire. But the deadly steel of the buccaneers' cutlasses at close quarters soon turned the tide. Almost half the garrison – seventy-four men – were killed; and before blowing up the fort, Morgan's pirates rescued eleven astonished English prisoners from the dungeons.

Slaughter of the hostages

The buccaneers continued their advance on Portobello, capturing other forts without resistance, and for the moment bypassing one in the town square where the Spanish governor had taken refuge. The sounds of firing had brought terrified townsfolk surging out into the streets, and now they ran for their lives, clutching precious possessions, pursued by blood-crazed groups of pirates. Looting, rape and slaughter were the order of the day.

Refusing to surrender, the governor of Portobello and his soldiers went on pouring musket shot into the narrow streets, where Morgan's men were running riot. Desperate measures were needed, and Morgan now came up with a hideously clever answer. Rounding up a group of Spanish friars and nuns, he ordered them to hoist onto their shoulders improvised scaling ladders knocked together from broad lengths of timber. Then he pushed them forward across the square surrounding the fort. Pistols and explosive fireballs at the ready, the pirates moved in cautiously behind their helpless hostages.

The Spanish governor, faced with a frightful dilemma, commanded his soldiers to keep raining fire down on the square as the ladders were placed in position. Dozens of innocent clergy fell dead as the buccaneers swarmed up the castle walls and over the ramparts. The Spanish soldiers threw away their guns and soon only the governor was left, fighting to the death. From the top of the smoking fortress, Henry Morgan looked down on Portobello, now completely at his mercy.

When the pillage and torture were over the buccaneers had collected some 250,000 pieces of eight, a large hoard of silver plate, hundreds of bales of silk stored in warehouses, and three hundred Negro slaves. They held the town for a month, routing a relief expedition, and sailed back victoriously to Port Royal. Morgan's casualties were eighteen men killed and thirty-two wounded.

The fireships of Maracaibo

Less than a year after the bloodthirsty raid on Portobello, Henry Morgan was seated with his officers around the dinner table on board his new flagship, H.M.S. *Oxford*, a fine three-masted frigate of three hundred tons. Suddenly there was a sinister rumbling from below decks. Within seconds, a tremendous explosion ripped the vessel apart. About two hundred crew members were killed instantly. Morgan himself was blown clean overboard. With a few dozen other survivors he struck out for shore. A pall of black smoke hung over the water, finally lifting to reveal the stern of the *Oxford* sinking slowly beneath the waves. Clinging to a spar, Morgan was at last fished out of the water, suffering only from minor cuts and bruises.

The explosion off the south coast of Hispaniola caused a temporary setback to Morgan's plans for an attack

The explosion of the Oxford

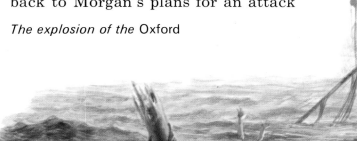

on Cartagena, another stronghold on the Spanish Main. So, with a reduced number of ships and men, he decided to choose a less formidable target. In the spring of 1669 he sailed for Maracaibo.

Only two years had passed since the citizens of that unfortunate town had been at the mercy of the dreaded L'Olonnois. They were to find Morgan almost as remorseless. Once the fortress at the lake entrance had been captured, Maracaibo and Gibraltar were again doomed, their streets deserted, houses abandoned, money and jewels snatched into hiding. Prisoners were tortured in order to make them tell where treasure had been concealed, and a vast amount of plunder amassed. After a month of riotous living the buccaneers left the scene of carnage, only to find that their exit route was effectively blocked by three Spanish warships.

Lacking the fire-power to take on the enemy frigates, Morgan decided to play for time. First he sent a message to the Spanish admiral.

'Pay me a ransom of 20,000 pieces of eight,' he wrote. 'If you do not agree I shall kill the hostages I am holding.'

The admiral dismissed Morgan's ultimatum with contempt. 'I am prepared to offer you free passage,' he replied, 'but only if you agree to hand over all the plunder you have taken, including gold, silver, jewels, prisoners and slaves. The only form of ransom I will pay will be in the form of cannon balls!'

Morgan made up his mind to make a dash for freedom. Whilst pretending to go on negotiating, he converted one of his smaller vessels into a fireship, placing explosives in the hold and strewing the decks with tar, brimstone and pitch. To give the impression that the ship was strongly armed, he set

Morgan's fireship routs the enemy at Maracaibo

his men working feverishly for several nights, constructing wooden cannons, painting imitation gun ports, and fashioning dummy wooden figures of sailors, their heads made of straw and adorned with colourful hats and garish neckerchiefs. A handful of volunteers then manoeuvred the vessel into the lake at dawn, heading straight for the enemy flagship, the *Magdalena*. Morgan's other ships followed in her wake.

The Spanish admiral was stunned by this display of bravado. Although a single accurate burst of cannon fire could easily have sent the small pirate vessel to the bottom, he held his fire, watching in disbelief as she ploughed steadily towards him. There was a gentle thud as the two ships touched. Then, recovering his senses, the admiral barked an order for his men to board the intruder. A few of the buccaneers fought a rearguard action while their companions leapt overboard. The last

man to escape lit the fuse. Minutes later, the fireship exploded. Flames immediately spread to the *Magdalena*, giving the admiral and his officers just enough time to lower the longboat and pull for shore. With the *Magdalena* a total loss, the second frigate, the *Marquesa*, cut her cable and made a bid for safety. She only succeeded in running aground. The third vessel, the *San Luis*, prudently surrendered to the pirates. Once more Henry Morgan sailed for Port Royal, laden with plunder and covered with glory.

Through the jungle to Panama

In 1670, the Spanish governor of the small island of Santa Catalina (Old Providence), about three hundred and fifty miles north of Panama, was woken from sleep with the unpleasant news that a huge pirate fleet was anchored offshore and that a bombardment could be expected any moment. Worse still,

it was believed that the ships were commanded by the terrible pirate, Henry Morgan. The garrison of the island was very small and the governor had no intention of dying a hero. He therefore sent a message to the English buccaneer, now boasting a new twenty-two-gun flagship, the *Satisfaction*, agreeing to surrender the island, but pleading with him to stage a mock attack, so that there could be no suggestion of a Spanish officer failing to do his duty. That night, Santa Catalina echoed to the crackling of musket fire. But Morgan, agreeing to save the governor's face, had ordered his men to use blank ammunition. Not surprisingly, the fort overlooking the harbour was taken without casualties on either side!

Morgan's attack was only a prelude to the most massive raid yet staged on the Spanish Main. He was in command of the largest buccaneer and privateer fleet ever seen in these waters – thirty-

Fifteenth- and sixteenth-century anchors

six ships (eight of them French, the rest English), carrying 1,846 men. The destination, decided by democratic vote when the ships were already at sea, was the fortified city of Panama, on the Pacific shore of the isthmus.

Santa Catalina provided timber for building a fleet of *pirogues* (canoes made from hollowed-out tree trunks) and three weeks later the invasion fleet dropped anchor off the estuary of the Chagres River. An advance force had already taken the fortress of San Lorenzo, perched on a high cliff overlooking the river. The opposition had been fierce and the casualties heavy, but when Morgan and the main fleet arrived the way to Panama lay open.

The Chagres was navigable for only forty miles. Then the invaders would

have to plunge through dense, uncharted jungle for a land attack on Panama. Even the first stage of the journey up the Chagres, with fourteen hundred buccaneers in seven sloops and a flotilla of small river boats and *pirogues*, turned out to be a nightmare. It lasted a week, as hunger, thirst, disease and swarms of insects sapped the men's strength and will. When the boats had to be abandoned, with 200 sick and weary pirates left behind to guard them, the main attack force struck out through the jungle, many of them scarcely able to stagger along. Each day reduced their numbers as men dropped dead along the trail from dysentery or sheer exhaustion.

The Indian tribes, which Morgan assumed to be friendly and likely to replenish the dwindling stocks of food and water, had silently drifted away into the depths of the forest. Soon the situation was desperate. After six days marching, many of the men were chewing the leather of their shoes, belts and pouches, and drinking brackish pool water. Total disaster was averted only when they stumbled unexpectedly on a supply of corn, which revived them enough to beat off Indian ambushes and give them new heart for the venture.

On the ninth day, following a night of welcome torrential rain, the skies cleared to reveal a distant strip of ocean, and a green valley with grazing cattle. The buccaneers rounded them up, killed as many as they needed for food, and set up camp for the night. In the morning they gazed out at the shimmering spires of Panama City.

Triumph and treachery

The Spaniards had by this time been forewarned and were fully prepared for the battle to come. Two squadrons of cavalry and four foot regiments were drawn up three miles outside the city walls, commanded by Don Juan Perez de Guzman, and outnumbering the buccaneers by more than two to one. In addition, a herd of several thousand wild cattle had been rounded up, the idea being that they would charge the enemy lines in support of the infantry. But Don Guzman's preparations were short-sighted on several counts. The marshy ground outside the town prevented him from deploying his cavalry, which was quickly routed by the pirates' accurate musket fire; and a few equally well-aimed shots so terrified the cattle that they stampeded, thundering back through the Spanish lines and scattering the foot forces drawn up in the rear.

Despite supporting bombardment from the town's cannons, two hours' fighting saw Morgan's rough-and-ready invading force completely victorious. The Spaniards fled back to the city and, after some half-hearted street fighting, abandoned it to the pirates. But before they left, they set fire to the town which had once been the pride of Spain's overseas empire.

By morning, Panama was a mass of charred ruins, but the plunder recovered from the mansions and warehouses that had escaped the flames was enough to have made the adventure worthwhile. The prize might have been considerably more; for a galleon carrying several million pieces of eight had prudently sailed out of the port a few hours before the battle. The frustrated buccaneers began torturing prisoners in a desperate attempt to locate more hidden loot. The situation threatened to get completely out of hand, but

Morgan called a halt to the drunken rampaging by tricking his men into believing that the enemy had poisoned all the stores of wine before leaving.

Morgan was ready for a Spanish counter-attack, but to his surprise and relief, it never came.

After three weeks in the ravaged city, the long trek back through the jungle began. The buccaneers took one hundred and seventy-five mules to transport the piles of gold and silver coins, plate, jewels and other valuables. Yet when the booty was finally shared out at Chagres, the pirates found, to their amazement and annoyance, that they were to receive a paltry sum of about £10 per head!

Judging by both Spanish and English estimates of the treasure taken from Panama, this seemed a pretty shabby reward for the thousand or so survivors of such a dangerous adventure. Where

A defence plan foiled

had the bulk of the treasure gone? It was generally assumed, although never proved, that Morgan deliberately swindled his men. One morning the buccaneers awoke to find that their captain had slipped away, with a few chosen colleagues and, presumably, most of the loot, leaving behind him only a reservoir of anger and bitter frustration.

The penitent pirate

Peace between England and Spain brought an end to Henry Morgan's buccaneering exploits but not to his career in the service of his country. Although he was brought back to England to stand trial (which never took place) for illegally raiding Panama, he returned, in 1674, to Jamaica as deputy-governor. Even now, complaints filtered through to London of his scandalous behaviour in local taverns, and there were rumours that he was still in touch with his buccaneer friends. But Sir Henry, as he was now entitled to be known, having been knighted by Charles II, was wealthy enough not to need new adventures; and, as if to prove that he was really on the side of law and order, he transformed himself into the most enthusiastic of pirate hunters. Once, when a Dutch vessel, manned mainly by Englishmen, entered Jamaican waters, Morgan captured her and dutifully handed over the crew to the Spaniards at Cartagena. He was not idly boasting when he reported, 'I have put to death, imprisoned and transported to the Spaniard for execution all English and Spanish pirates that I could get.'

At the age of fifty-three, Sir Henry Morgan died, his health ruined by dissipation. Exquemelin, who claimed to have served under him on the Panama expedition, did not have a kind word to say of him in *The Buccaneers of America*, but the citizens of Port Royal gave him a lavish funeral.

In 1692, four years after Morgan's death, Port Royal was racked by an earthquake. Some twenty thousand people died and more than half of the town literally crumbled into the sea. Although it continued to be an important trading centre, its great days of piracy were over. Yet the memory of the swashbuckling buccaneers of Port Royal lingered on. Three centuries later, in the harbour of the thriving city of Kingston, built on the site of the old pirate town, treasure seekers are busy exploring the ocean bed for relics of those violent, colourful years; and discoveries of gold coins and other precious objects suggest that tales of sunken treasure in the Caribbean may not be pure fancy after all!

CHAPTER THREE
Adventure and misadventure in the South Seas

Ten years had passed since Henry Morgan captured Panama City. Now, on a spring day in 1680, five Spanish treasure galleons lay at anchor off the Pacific coast of Panama. The ships were deserted, for their crews had been crammed aboard three barks which were heading out of the harbour to challenge a little fleet of canoes and rowing boats cruising just outside the bay. The small Spanish warships carried cannon, and the two hundred men on board were armed to the teeth. Word had reached Panama that a force of English buccaneers had crossed the isthmus into the Pacific and were planning a new raid on the city. But as the Spanish admiral commanding the barks took measure of the enemy, he must have felt that the authorities were panicking needlessly. Apart from the small boats, which could not possibly hold more than a few dozen fighting men, there were no stronger support vessels in sight. This, he told himself, was going to be ludicrously easy. If these were real buccaneers he would teach them a lesson.

Captain John Coxon and his men were indeed buccaneers, and they watched

61

the three sailing ships bearing down on them with a feeling of grim determination, but little hope. Having endured so much in the past month the prospect of a clean, quick death in a sea battle held no fears. A force of more than three hundred had trekked through the jungle after sacking Porto-

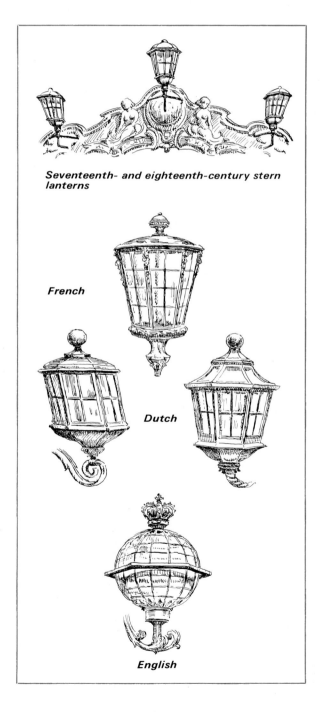

Seventeenth- and eighteenth-century stern lanterns

French

Dutch

English

bello, on the Caribbean shore of the isthmus of Panama. Many were dead, others had sailed off in search of a prize, and today there were only sixty-eight men left to face a vastly superior enemy. But they still had their knives and muskets, and by now they were desperate.

In a running battle lasting five hours the tiny force of buccaneers achieved the impossible. Rowing close in for the hand-to-hand fighting which they preferred, they killed more than one hundred Spaniards, including the admiral, brought the enemy barks to a standstill and forced the survivors to surrender. The galleons were now at the mercy of the pirates. All the ships were stripped of cargo, two set on fire and sent to the bottom, two left alone, and the last, the four hundred-ton *Trinidad*, boarded and converted into a new flagship. Ironically, she was the very ship that had eluded Morgan at the sack of Panama City.

This was the first real success in an expedition which had been badly planned and then dogged by ill luck. The decision to raid Panama again, reviving memories of Drake and Morgan, had been unanimous. The West Indies were no longer happy hunting grounds for pirates. Both the English and French governments, for political reasons, were determined to sweep the Caribbean clean; and now that the Manila galleons were regularly plying the Pacific route, it seemed logical for buccaneers to look for plunder in the South Seas and on the west coast of South America. Such men, who were prepared to risk the terrors of the tropical jungle as well as face the steel and shot of the enemy, still had only one objective. A survivor of Coxon's party admitted quite openly and cheerfully that ' . . . it was gold that was the bait that tempted a pack of merry boys of us.'

Muddles and mistakes

The exploits of Coxon and other pirate commanders such as Richard Sawkins, Bartholomew Sharp and Edward Davis were undeniably colourful but they yielded little in terms of profit and prestige. What these captains lacked was the flair for leadership which Drake and Morgan possessed. They were brave but they were unable to inspire their crews. Despite occasional successes, one gets the impression of muddle and incompetence, of mistrust and betrayal, of frustration and failure. The reason that their adventures make such exciting reading is that serving under them at various times were three young buccaneers, who kept notes and diaries which gave fascinating first-hand accounts of the actions in which they took part. Lionel Wafer was a young surgeon, Basil Ringrose had been an apprentice on a plantation, and William Dampier was a restless adventurer who was later to win fame as an author and explorer, making three journeys round the world.

The squabbles began immediately after the victory off the Panama coast. Coxon, already criticized for his poor record, marched back across the isthmus with seventy men, and Richard Sawkins, described by Ringrose as 'a valiant and generous-spirited man', was elected in his place. Sawkins was killed in a futile attack on the coastal town of Pueblo Nuevo and was succeeded by Bartholomew Sharp, who promised £1,000 in plunder to every buccaneer that followed him. By the time the raiders reached the deserted

'We parted with the richest booty . . .

island of Juan Fernández, around Christmas of 1680, not only had they received hardly any treasure but they faced the grim prospect of a winter passage around Cape Horn. The men deposed Sharp and appointed as captain John Watling, a man who insisted on strict Sabbath observance, yet proved unsurpassed for personal cruelty. Soon the buccaneers were begging

Sharp to resume command, and by good fortune Watling was killed in a disastrous raid on the Chilean port of Arica.

Within a few days they were at loggerheads once more. A group of forty-four buccaneers, including Dampier and Wafer, sailed 600 miles north in a frail longboat, intending to return to the Caribbean by land across Panama. The remaining seventy, loyal to Sharp, also turned north, zigzagged south again, and finally captured two treasure ships. The second was carrying seven hundred silver ingots from the Peruvian mines; and at that point something happened which seems to sum up the inexperience and recklessness of so many of these South Seas buccaneers.

Unbelievably, the pirates tossed all but one of the ingots overboard, assuming they were worthless tin! The man who kept his for moulding into bullets later sold it for £75. As one rueful crew member put it, 'We parted with the richest booty we got in the whole voyage through our own ignorance and laziness.'

Lionel Wafer and the Indians

Deep in the heart of the Panama jungle five white men, ragged and weak from illness and hunger, listened to the torrential rain lashing the flimsy roof of their palm-thatched hut and resigned themselves to their fate. After weeks of aimless wandering through the rain forest they had found temporary refuge

Lionel Wafer's first encounter with the Cuna Indians

leg with their home-made paste of herbs, but for some reason they were far from friendly. His friends were allowed to roam around the village but wherever they went they were subjected to jeers and curses. The small amount of food they were given consisted mainly of unripe plantain fruit which was difficult to digest. And now doubt had turned to grim certainty. Wafer had heard rumours that these Indians preferred to roast their victims alive rather than shed their blood. In a clearing, only a few yards from the hut, a group of naked, brightly tattooed warriors had ominously heaped up branches and twigs for a ritual execution.

Next morning an Indian, obviously a tribal chief, appeared at the hut entrance and the five men prepared for the worst. To their joy, however, the Indians seemed to have altered their attitude completely. Far from being hostile, they now showed the utmost friendliness. By signs, the chief made them understand that he would give them guides and send them on their way. Astonished and delighted at this sudden reversal of fortune, Wafer and his friends decided to leave at once.

The Englishmen hoped that the guides would take them to a point where they might pick up the trail of the main body of buccaneers. But again the Indians proved unpredictable. Evidently acting upon instructions, they abandoned the white men after a few days, leaving them once more hopelessly lost and almost without food. They staggered on, eating nuts and berries, until they came to a river. This revived their spirits, for with a couple of makeshift rafts they could float down to the sea. Hopefully, the river might even lead to the Caribbean. But

in a village of primitive Cuna Indians. One of the white men was scarcely able to hobble along, his knee shattered by an accidental explosion of gunpowder. Wracked by pain, Lionel Wafer was unrecognizable as the high-spirited young buccaneer who had parted company from Bartholomew Sharp six months previously.

After the accident, Wafer had begged the other buccaneers to leave him and to continue their journey across Panama to the relative safety of the Caribbean. All but four had agreed. As he lay on his pallet of leaves and straw, Wafer wondered how many of them had managed to get through. For himself and his companions the prospects were grim. True, the Indians had patched up his

during the night a tropical rainstorm swept the frail rafts away and left them in a state of utter despair and misery. By the time they hit upon a forest trail leading to another Indian village they were too weary to care what happened, stumbling into a clearing and throwing themselves on the mercy of the astonished villagers.

Their fate remained in the balance. Although these Indians were friendly enough, they insisted on paddling their honoured guests straight back to the village which had first prepared a funeral pyre for them and then provided them with guides who had left them to die in the jungle. Not knowing whether they would be received with bouquets or brickbats, they were immensely relieved to find their hosts once again in

An astonishing reunion

a good mood; and when Wafer used his medical knowledge to cure the chief's favourite wife, who had fallen sick, he was hailed as a miracle-worker. For three months he and his four companions lived with the Indians. It gave Wafer a marvellous opportunity to study their customs and learn some words of their strange language. Eventually he was fluent enough to explain that they would like to be conducted to the Caribbean shore of the isthmus to look for their shipmates. The chief, now all smiles, agreed and this time personally escorted them to the coast. There they were reunited with their fellow buccaneers, who had long given them up for dead. It took some time to recognize Lionel Wafer, for he was dressed for the occasion in the traditional costume of his Indian friends – just a loincloth and a colourful pattern of body paints!

Discord among allies

Captain Edward Davis, the English commander of the thirty-six-gun *Bachelor's Delight*, was seething with rage. He had just missed a golden opportunity, nothing less than the capture of the Lima treasure fleet. Never again, he vowed, would he trust the word of a Frenchman.

They had known the odds against them – ten rickety, poorly provisioned buccaneer ships (only two of them carrying cannon) facing fourteen fully equipped Spanish vessels, six of them strongly armed. His own force of eleven hundred men was made up of about seven hundred Englishmen and four hundred Frenchmen, and he reckoned that the enemy had at least 2,500 sailors and soldiers at their disposal. But if he had only been able to count on the support of a reliable ally, things might have gone well. As it was . . .

Davis felt he was justified in assuming supreme command. The Frenchman had grumbled, but having reluctantly agreed, it was his duty to obey orders. When the battle had begun, the French ships had kept safely out of range when their intervention could have tipped the balance. As a result it was the English ships that had been holed by enemy gunfire, Englishmen who had been killed and wounded. And the galleons had escaped.

A series of quick, surprise attacks on the mainland might still help to restore confidence and English prestige, thought Davis, but this time he would go it alone, without the 'help' of any cowardly Frenchmen.

Captain Grognier, for his part, was equally angry and frustrated. The entire action had been badly planned and weakly executed, thanks to his English allies. The arrogance of Edward Davis was intolerable. By what right had he placed himself in command of the joint venture in the first place? And having done so he had added insult to injury by allotting Grognier and his four hundred Frenchmen only two ships, neither of which was armed! The whole thing was ridiculous and Davis's tactics in the futile engagement with the Spanish ships were suicidal. He had done his best in support but once it was obvious that the treasure fleet had escaped what was the point of sacrificing his two useless ships and his fighting men? At least his force was more or less intact. It might still be worth trying their luck on the mainland. But this time he would be in charge and solely responsible.

His own men, he admitted, were not

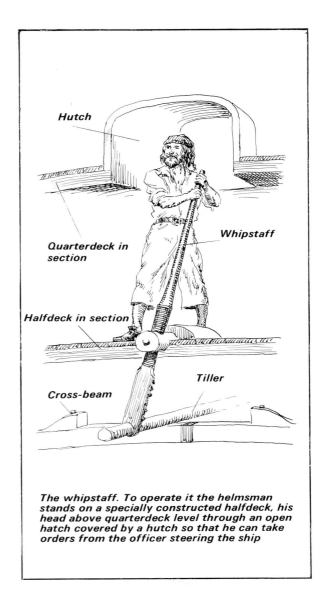

The whipstaff. To operate it the helmsman stands on a specially constructed halfdeck, his head above quarterdeck level through an open hatch covered by a hutch so that he can take orders from the officer steering the ship

exactly gentlemen adventurers. If brute force had to be used to win the day he could set as good an example as the next man; and in the heat of battle how could he prevent a little looting and raping? But the English were worse, little better than heathens. At least the Spaniards were good Catholics, like most of his own men. Those Protestant English savages had no respect for the true faith and would sack and burn a church as cheerfully as a palace. No, he promised himself, there would be no more 'alliances'. What he and his men won, they would keep.

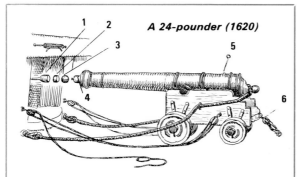

A 24-pounder (1620)

1. Ramrod rams charge home. 2. Cotton wad
3. Ball. 4. Powder charge in cotton wrapping.
5. Priming wire proves charge is rammed home.
6. Deck tackle used to 'run in'.

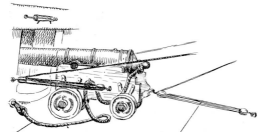

7. Breeching now loose. 8. Deck tackle keeps
gun on true line.

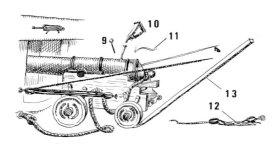

9. Priming wire pierces cotton wrapping of
charge. 10. Priming powder poured in. 11. Slow
match to ignite. 12. Deck tackle now free.
13. Hand spikes to adjust lateral alignment

Gun fires and 'runs in' on recoil. Backward
movement arrested by breeching. Barrel is
cleaned with water, using a cleaning rod with
lamb's wool head. Gun is now ready for
reloading in sequence shown above

William Dampier, on board the English flagship, agreed with his captain as to where the blame lay, and in his written report of the engagement was highly critical of the French lack of cooperation. Raveneau de Lussan, on the other hand, recorded the French point of view with equal warmth, insisting that the English were the principal culprits. Whatever the truth, it was hardly an inspired example of allies working with a common purpose. After that French and English went their own ways, but as might have been predicted, they met with little success. The Spaniards realized, on the sound principle of 'divide and conquer', that they were more than a match for any inexperienced invading force which could be split up and dealt with separately. Now they simply sat back and watched the 'allies' proceed to cut their own throats!

Captain Davis probably came off better than most of the other South Sea buccaneers. With Lionel Wafer jotting down events in his journals, Davis cruised up and down the South American coast, sacked the town of Guayaquil and brought the *Bachelor's Delight* back to the West Indies in the spring of 1688. Although King James II had proclaimed a general pardon for any pirates who were prepared to give themselves up, Davis and Wafer decided to settle in Virginia and were promptly arrested. It was touch and go as to whether they would be executed, but eventually they were freed.

Captain Grognier met a more violent end. Despite his resolve to fight alone in future, he joined forces with an English buccaneer named Townley. Together they proceeded to blaze a trail of destruction through Panama and down the South American coast, including another sacking of the hapless town of Guayaquil. Their raids were usually distinguished by the wholesale torture and slaughter of prisoners, and when both men finally died of their wounds few people, friends or foes, mourned them.

William Dampier parted company with Davis and threw in his lot with Captain Charles Swan on the *Cygnet*. Swan was not much of a leader and met near-disaster in an attack on the small town of Santa Pecaque in February, 1686. Returning from the raid with some plunder, Swan's men were strung out at such long intervals that they seemed to be inviting a counter-attack. Somewhere along the trail the buccaneers were quietly ambushed and fifty-four of them slashed to ribbons. Among the dead was Basil Ringrose. Swan, with a relief force, arrived too late. The Spaniards had melted away into the forest

and Swan could do nothing but survey the grisly scene in anguish.

Swan decided to renounce buccaneering and sailed the *Cygnet* across the Pacific. He was drowned in the Philippines but Dampier, recording the voyage in his journals, remained with the *Cygnet* until she reached New Holland (Australia). Then he slipped ashore one night, clutching his sea-chest, his compass and his precious papers. Always eager for adventure, Dampier took another three years to complete his first round-the-world journey, publishing his colourful experiences in a book entitled *A New Voyage Round the World*.

The high-spirited French buccaneer, Raveneau de Lussan, had been among the Anglo-French party that sacked Guayaquil. Later he made his way with a group of his countrymen, first on foot and then down river, from the Pacific coast of Honduras to the Caribbean.

The end of Lussan's journey

Lussan boards ship for Petit Goave

plus wealth. They slipped away early one morning and he never saw them again. Probably they died in the jungle. But the decision saved his life. After a hazardous journey of torrid days and freezing nights, the continual risk of Spanish attacks and the ravages of disease and hunger, Lussan was grateful to be spared to see once more the blue waters of the Caribbean and the friendly harbour of Petit Goave. And he too published his exciting story in a book called *Journal of a Voyage to the South Sea with the American Filibusters*.

The real Robinson Crusoe

In January 1709 two privateer vessels, the three hundred and twenty-ton *Duke* and the two hundred and fifty-ton *Duchess* battled their way around Cape Horn. Lashed by snow, sleet and towering waves formed by the clashing currents of two oceans, the ships finally reached calmer waters. Two weeks later they were lying off the shore of Juan Fernández. Here they could be repaired and take on provisions. Many crew members were suffering from scurvy, due to the lack of fresh fruit and vegetables, and now they could rest and recuperate.

The ships were commanded by Captain Woodes Rogers, a capable, decisive young man who carried an official commission (since England was now at war both with France and Spain) to attack ships on his voyage round the world. Since his earlier buccaneering adventures, Dampier had been engaged in more serious voyages of exploration, but his stubborn nature and quarrelsome temperament did not suit him for command of this expedition. Nobody questioned his skill as a navigator,

Most of the buccaneers were weighted down with treasure, but Lussan prudently changed his heavy pieces of eight into pearls and other jewels. Since the load was still too bulky, he divided his booty among a number of companions, on the understanding that they would return it to him if and when they reached their destination. Temptation was too great for the men who had been entrusted with Lussan's sur-

however, and he and Rogers made a good team.

As night fell, Rogers and Dampier, from the deck of the *Duke*, peered at the dark outline of the island, trying to decide the safest place to land. Just as the ship's pinnace was being lowered overboard, Rogers caught his breath in surprise. A bright light, evidently a fire, had suddenly blazed up from the shore. Rogers hesitated. This could mean that a French ship was lurking at anchor in the bay. He could not risk sending men ashore in the darkness. Cancelling his order for the pinnace to be taken out, Rogers decided to wait until morning and went below.

Soon after dawn, having satisfied himself that there was no enemy ship in sight, Rogers sent the pinnace ashore with a strong landing party. Although there was no sign of life on the beach he could not be sure that there was not an ambush in store. An anxious hour passed, the pinnace bobbing empty in the shallows. Then the men reappeared, there was a flurry of activity on the beach and, minutes later, the pinnace was heading back to the *Duke*.

Rogers watched the boat creeping nearer. A head count showed that nobody was missing. In fact there seemed to be one man too many. Could it be a prisoner? There had been no sounds of firing. A native? But the island was known to be uninhabited. Rogers was puzzled.

One by one the crew of the *Duke* clambered aboard. The stranger they had brought back was a very odd-looking individual indeed. His hair was matted and dishevelled, his long beard untrimmed and straggling, his face deeply lined, although he did not seem to be an old man. The tattered clothes he wore and the makeshift cap on his head appeared to be made of goatskin. He stuttered badly, the words muffled and incomprehensible. Perhaps the man was crazy. Yet there was something in his appearance, some trick of the voice, that attracted Dampier's attention. He took a closer look. Where had he seen this man before? Try as he might, he could not make any sense out of that torrent of meaningless words. Were they English? Almost, but not quite. Some dialect perhaps. Irish, Scots? Yes, that was it – a pronounced Scottish intonation! Suddenly the light flooded through. He grabbed the man by the arm, closely scanning his features. Then he gasped with amazement. 'By heaven,' he exclaimed, 'you must be Alexander Selkirk!' The man recoiled as if he had been hit; but there was a flicker of recognition in his eyes.

Dampier remembered the man well. Blunt, argumentative, never afraid to

The rescue of Alexander Selkirk

speak his mind, Alexander Selkirk had served as quartermaster on board the *Cinque Ports*, an English privateer that had sailed these waters more than four years ago. Dampier too had been on this expedition, a crew member of the sister-ship *St George*. Selkirk had quarrelled violently with his captain, Thomas Stradling, claiming that the *Cinque Ports* was unseaworthy and demanding to be put ashore on Juan Fernández. Stradling had agreed. It was fortunate for Selkirk that he was well provided with tools, books and ammunition. Expecting only a short stay on the island, he was to spend four years and four months there in total isolation. Not having communicated with anyone for all that time, he had practically lost his powers of speech.

Selkirk had been highly resourceful in keeping alive. He had plenty of fresh water and ate goats' meat, crawfish, vegetables and fruit. He had built a couple of huts, complete with simple utensils and furniture, but apart from animals he had not seen a living creature from the time Stradling sailed away until the day a shipload of English sailors tramped over the sand to rescue him. Now his confidence gradually returned and he began forming words and sentences. Within a few weeks he was talking freely.

Woodes Rogers was so impressed by Selkirk's remarkable tale of survival that he transcribed it into his journal. He later included the story in his exciting book entitled *A Cruising Voyage Round the World*. Rogers tells how the castaway hunted goats on foot after running out of ammunition, how he seasoned his meat with pimentoes and black pepper, adding turnips and cabbages as fresh vegetables. He tamed and bred goats and also raised cats, which swiftly dealt with the many rats, and he soon came to terms with his solitude.

Selkirk was later given the command of a captured Spanish prize, and the whole fleet returned to England in October 1711. The journalist Richard Steele was so intrigued by Selkirk's story that he wrote an article; and it was either this paper or Woodes Rogers's account which inspired Daniel Defoe to write *The Life and Surprising Adventures of Robinson Crusoe*, published in 1719. Selkirk never met Defoe and won neither fame nor fortune. Two years after the best-selling novel appeared, he died at sea.

The Nonsuch *pounds the French frigates into surrender*

CHAPTER FOUR

French corsairs of the Channel coast

As the two English men-of-war bore swiftly down on the convoy of French merchantmen, Jean Bart, captain of the forty-gun frigate *Les Jeux*, signalled his decision to his second-in-command Claude de Forbin, commander of *La Railleuse*. They would stand and fight. It might prove to be nothing better than a stubborn rearguard action against superior strength, but it would give twenty merchant ships, with their cargoes of gunpowder, a chance to slip through the English Channel to their destination, the port of Brest.

England and France, lately allies, were now at war with each other. On this May morning of 1689 Jean Bart, corsair turned privateer, faced the gravest challenge of his seagoing career. His plan was to leave the second English warship to give chase to the convoy and to lead the two frigates in a boarding attempt on the larger man-of-war, the *Nonsuch*.

The tactics were sound but the plan was upset by a stroke of bad luck, and it was this alone that upset the strategy. Suddenly the wind veered around, preventing *Les Jeux* and *La Railleuse* from getting in close enough. The powerful guns of the *Nonsuch* had time to find their range and as the frigates returned the fire, honours were about even. Gradually however, the tide of battle changed. To Bart's dismay, he saw that the guns of the second English warship had silenced those of the only three merchantmen that were armed. The latter were now in full flight and the French frigates were caught in a deadly hail of enemy crossfire.

For three hours the battle off the south coast of the Isle of Wight raged fiercely. Although both Bart and Forbin were wounded, they carried on fighting until masts and rigging were smashed, poops and forecastles shot away, powder and guns immobilized. By that time all but a few dozen of the frigates' crews were dead or wounded. There was no alternative but to surrender.

Meanwhile, the English had also suffered heavy losses. The captains and officers of both warships had been killed in the battle. But there was great glee in London when news came through of the capture of two of the most renowned and dangerous French corsairs of the age.

The cabin boy and the count

Claude de Forbin, recording the humiliating episode, years later, in his *Mémoires*, was highly indignant of the offensive way in which his captors treated him. The moment he stepped aboard the *Nonsuch* he was stripped naked and rigged out with a common sailor's jersey, ragged breeches and a ridiculous woollen cap. Jean Bart, on the other hand, was permitted to keep his blue and gold uniform, evidently because he spoke a few words of English. It was a trivial enough incident, but enough to fan the flames of jealousy and hatred that had been raging in Forbin's heart.

The French Minister of the Navy had congratulated himself on engaging the services of two of the most experienced corsair captains of the day, but he was taking a risk in putting Bart in overall command and expecting the two men to work amicably together. It was like putting a bull and a tiger in the same cage.

The capture of Bart and Forbin

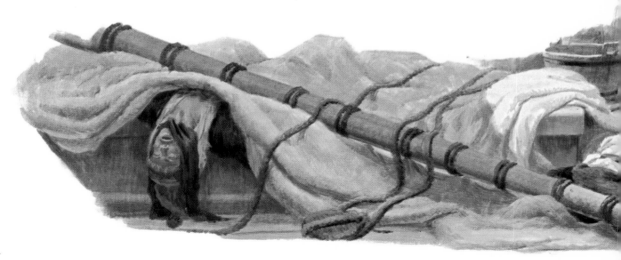

Seafaring was in the blood of Jean Bart, the most celebrated of the Dunkirk corsairs. For over a century, the men of his family had been privateers – an honourable occupation in a town whose history of seafaring stretched back to the twelfth century – and at twelve years old he had begun his career as cabin boy on a small coastguard vessel. At sixteen, he had seen action with the famous Dutch Admiral de Ruyter, but, when France went to war with Holland, he had the chance to combine service to his country with personal profit, gaining rapid promotion. While England remained neutral, Jean Bart simply extended his range, adding English merchant ships to his tally of Dutch prizes. And when, in 1689, the War of the Grand Alliance broke out, with France engaged on land and at sea against England, Holland and their allies, Bart was an obvious choice for a high naval command.

Six years younger than Bart, Claude de Forbin's background and upbringing had been very different. He came from a noble family in Provence and had seen service abroad, including two years at the court of Siam. Although his duties were not too demanding, the King had conferred upon him the impressive title of Grand Admiral of Siam, and Forbin was scrupulous in signing his letters and documents in that way.

Conscious of his aristocratic traditions, Forbin was quick-tempered, quarrelsome and conceited. He was respected but not much liked. Bart, on the other hand, was blunt and outspoken, mixing easily with men of simple origins. Forbin, for all his faults, was certainly a brave officer. But why should he, a nobleman, take orders from an upstart commoner? In the years to come, becoming more and more irritated by Bart's glowing reputation, he would never miss an opportunity to belittle his colleague and glorify his own exploits. But now, for better or worse, their destinies were linked.

The break for freedom

When the notorious corsairs reached Plymouth they were politely wined and dined by their English captors, Bart chatting light-heartedly with his

'hosts', Forbin glowering at the foot of the table, suspecting that he was deliberately being treated as a laughing-stock. But once the civilities were over, they were both locked in a room of a local tavern. The windows were barred and guards were posted outside the door.

The English seemed curiously undecided whether to regard Bart and Forbin as dangerous prisoners or as privileged guests. It was rather foolish, in the interests of security, for them to allow the corsair captains to share their room with two Dunkirk cabin boys or to appoint a sympathetic naval surgeon to run about the town carrying messages and attending to all their needs. After a couple of days, a cousin of Jean Bart, who happened to be staying in Plymouth (he was serving with the Spanish who were, at this time, allies of England), discovered where the captives were being held, contacted the surgeon and bribed him to smuggle in a file. It was a simple task to cut through the flimsy bars of the make-shift prison and escape during the night.

The resourceful cousin had meanwhile cornered a drunken Norwegian sailor in a local tavern and commandeered from him a dinghy, with oars, compass and provisions. Silently he

The corsairs return to St Malo

guided the escaped corsairs down to the jetty. It was still dark when they cast off. Even at this critical point there was a heated argument. 'I can't possibly row,' Forbin announced, 'because my bad arm is still terribly painful. Get the lads to help you with the oars. I'll do the steering.'

Jean Bart had no choice. He rowed almost non-stop for fifty-three hours, pausing only now and then to take a bite of bread and sausage or swig of beer. The boys took turns with the second oar while Forbin, at the rudder, dozed off at intervals. Fortunately the sea was calm and during the first crucial hours they were safely shrouded in the mist.

On the morning of their third day in the Channel, Bart brought the dinghy safely into the little fishing harbour of Erquy. Soon afterwards they were given a heroes' welcome by the excited populace of St Malo. This picturesque town, with its twelfth century ramparts, was a famous corsair base, rivalling Dunkirk. Today the townsfolk waved and cheered as if Bart and Forbin were their native sons.

Bart was tired and dejected. Conscious of having failed in his mission, he wanted only to get home. But Forbin, more astute, headed for Versailles to give his own version of events to a delighted Minister of the Navy. When he repeated the exciting story to King Louis XIV, emphasizing the leading role he had played in the action, Forbin was rewarded with promotion.

Justice was done in the end. When an influential friend of Bart's suggested that Forbin might not deserve full credit for the brave exploit, Bart too was promoted and given a handsome monetary reward.

The upstart Danes

A year after their escape from England, Bart and Forbin, still uneasy comrades in arms, put into the port of Bergen, then under Danish occupation. They had in tow a number of Dutch herring boats, which they claimed as legal prizes after a one-sided engagement in the North Sea. For once, the two Frenchmen were in agreement. It had been a satisfactory affair. They had forced the Dutch skippers either to pay a ransom in return for safe passage or to watch helplessly as their vessels were set on fire and sunk. But now they ran into unexpected trouble.

The governor of Bergen happened to be a German, with no love for Frenchmen and a particular contempt for corsairs. He immediately confiscated the captured Dutch vessels. Forbin was especially infuriated by this high-handed behaviour and was soon reproaching Bart for not taking a firmer stand. How dare this nobody accuse officers of the French navy of being common pirates? If Bart preferred to spend all his time getting drunk in the Bergen taverns, he (Forbin) would certainly do something about it.

Putting on his haughtiest aristocratic air, Forbin angrily accused the governor of insulting the King of France by confiscating their prizes. Darkly, he hinted at terrible revenge. The governor, overcome by confusion and indecision, tried to shift the blame on an underling. When it became obvious that he was not prepared to countermand his orders, Forbin and Bart decided to take matters into their own hands. They boarded the impounded vessels, routing the Danish guards.

The Frenchmen were furious to find that the Danes had meantime ransacked the ships. Although the governor tried to make amends by arresting the officer responsible for the looting and throwing him into prison, this was not the end of the affair. The Bergen episode flared up into an international incident as the French ambassador in Copenhagen lodged an official protest with the Danish government. When Bart and Forbin got back to France, after a storm-tossed voyage during which provisions ran so low that they almost died of starvation, they were ordered to Versailles to give their accounts of the events at Bergen. Once again, Forbin claimed full credit for the successful outcome of the tricky negotiations. But it was Bart, much to Forbin's disgust, who was officially congratulated and rewarded.

That was the last time the two men sailed together into battle. Bart covered himself with further glory in 1694 at the Battle of the Texel, routing a squadron of Dutch warships and capturing the enemy flagship, and continued to wreak

Section of three-decker, showing guns run out, hammocks slung, stowage of stores and powder in hold

havoc with merchant shipping before the war ended a few years later. And for his part in the engagement, Bart was honoured by being created Chevalier, thereby claiming equal noble rank with his rival Claude de Forbin!

When war loomed once more in 1702, Bart was ready to go to sea again but was struck down by pleurisy before taking up his new command. Forbin, however, lived to see more action during the War of the Spanish Succession. His finer qualities of personal courage and bold leadership brought him renown in several battles. But another famous corsair captain was soon to find him as difficult and embarrassing a colleague as he had been when he sailed alongside the hero of Dunkirk, Jean Bart.

The superstitious corsair

As the people lining the quay at St Malo shoved and elbowed one another to get a clearer view of the heroes, Jean Bart and Claude de Forbin (both exhausted from their Channel ordeal but obviously delighted to be on French soil once more), a teen-aged boy gazed down from his vantage point on the town walls and made a silent promise. His eyes glistened and his heart fluttered with excitement as the yelling, flag-waving crowd milled around the two small figures on the quay below. 'One day,' he thought to himself, 'they will be cheering for me!'

As the younger son of a prosperous St Malo shipowner, René Duguay-Trouin had been expected to become a priest. But what kind of career was that for an adventure-loving boy who, from earliest childhood, had identified himself with the corsair traditions of his home town? He thrilled to the very

From dream to reality

sound and smell of the sea and could hardly wait for the day when he would be old enough to sail out of St Malo in a handsome frigate to serve his country and seek his fortune. Now, at sixteen, that time had come.

René Duguay-Trouin was no idle daydreamer. Only a few months after the memorable homecoming of Bart and Forbin, he was at sea and in action for the first time against a Dutch merchantman. By the age of eighteen he had proved his personal bravery and gained his first command. Two years later, his boyhood ambition was on the way to being achieved. The summer of 1693 saw him cruising in the Channel, now the commander of the royal frigate *L'Hercule*.

The past few weeks had been successful in terms of prizes – six English and two Dutch merchant ships captured, with no French casualties. But now *L'Hercule* was jammed tight with prisoners, food and water were running low and his crew were interested in only one thing, getting back to St Malo as soon as possible. He had announced his decision to stay at sea a while longer, and had already taken the highly unpopular step of cutting their rations by one third. To quieten their grumbling he had promised them that when they took another prize they would be allowed to loot it at will. 'I knew in my heart,' he wrote later in his *Mémoires*, 'that it was unfair to cut their rations but I was driven by an inner voice which made it impossible for me to do otherwise . . . I knew too that it was against the regulations to promise them all the booty . . . My only excuse is that I was very young at the time.'

Duguay-Trouin had heard this 'inner voice' before. Superstitious by nature, he claimed he could sense what was going to happen next. On this occasion he was convinced that his luck was about to change. But he had promised his men a prize within eight days: and, after a week's inactivity, he realized that they were on the brink of mutiny. That night, sleeping in his cabin, he had a vivid dream. Two large, fully-rigged vessels were looming up on the horizon, preparing to attack. Awaking with a start, he rushed on deck and there, less than a mile away, were the billowing white sails of two real ships. Pausing only long enough to make certain they were not French, Duguay-Trouin ordered the call to quarters sounded. At the roll of the drums the well-trained crew sprang to battle stations. Minutes later, flame and smoke belched into the night. Shot answered shot but gradually, one after another, the guns of the enemy ships fell silent. Finally the flags of surrender were run up the mizzen-masts. At daybreak, Duguay-Trouin sent his crew aboard. The ships that had fought such a bitter duel in the darkness were armed East Indiamen with valuable cargoes of gold, silver and sugar. Duguay-Trouin had kept his promise. More than ever, the strange incident convinced him that there must be some mysterious power watching over his fortunes.

A prison romance

A year later, by an extraordinary stroke of irony, René Duguay-Trouin was planning his escape from an English prison in Plymouth, the very same town from which his boyhood heroes (Bart and Forbin) had made their departure five years previously. For he had been captured after a fierce sea battle in which his new flagship *La Diligente* had been outgunned by six English warships. Struck on the head by a piece of flying shrapnel, the young captain had been unconscious aboard the enemy vessel and recovered to find himself bound for Plymouth.

During his first few days in England, Duguay-Trouin was treated with astonishing leniency and was allowed to wander the streets of the town unguarded. In one of the local taverns he met a pretty English girl and was soon head-over-heels in love. Then, quite unexpectedly, he was arrested and thrown into prison. Fortunately his new girl friend was permitted to visit him every day and it was she who helped him complete escape plans.

One of Duguay-Trouin's guards happened to be a French refugee and he too

Night escape from Plymouth

was soon captivated by the charms of the beautiful English visitor, so he decided to tell his prisoner about it. Duguay-Trouin, resourceful as ever, promised to help the lovelorn guard. 'I will be your go-between,' he volunteered. 'Write her a letter and I will personally make sure it is delivered to her. But I can't talk freely with her here in my cell. Let me out for a couple of hours so that I can meet her in the inn next door.'

The guard delightedly agreed. 'What,' he asked, 'can I do for you in return?' 'Just a small thing,' replied his prisoner, 'simply to deliver a letter to a friend.' Torn between love and duty, the French guard promised to fulfil his side of the bargain.

Before being locked up, Duguay-Trouin had become friendly, in a local tavern, with the captain of a Swedish ship anchored in the harbour. Now he had written to his drinking companion, asking him for his help in a bold escape plan. Discipline at the prison was so lax that the Swedish captain was able to send one of his trusted officers to see Duguay-Trouin. In return, Duguay-Trouin's own quartermaster, imprisoned in the same cell, was allowed to stroll down to the harbour to make the necessary arrangements. Soon he had fixed a price with the Swedish captain for the purchase of a dinghy, together with muskets, oars and sufficient provisions for an escape party of four. The ship's doctor and Duguay-Trouin's personal valet, who were also being held prisoner, completed the group.

Everything went smoothly. As soon as the guard saw his sweetheart enter the inn, he released his prisoner. After a tearful parting with the girl, Duguay-Trouin clambered over the rear garden wall of the tavern and made off with his companions, who had been allowed out for their customary afternoon stroll. The Swedes were punctually at the rendezvous, the boat was ready. From now on it was literally plain sailing. After rowing all night, the Frenchmen were out of sight of land. No English ships spotted the tiny boat and three days later, weary but exultant, the escaped prisoners put into St Malo and received a tumultuous welcome.

Duguay-Trouin described this dramatic episode in his *Mémoires*. What he never discovered, and what we shall never know, is what happened to that over-trustful guard and the pretty English girl who helped to free him and perhaps save his life.

A brother sacrificed

As the *Sans Pareil* cruised off the west coast of Spain on a late summer morn-

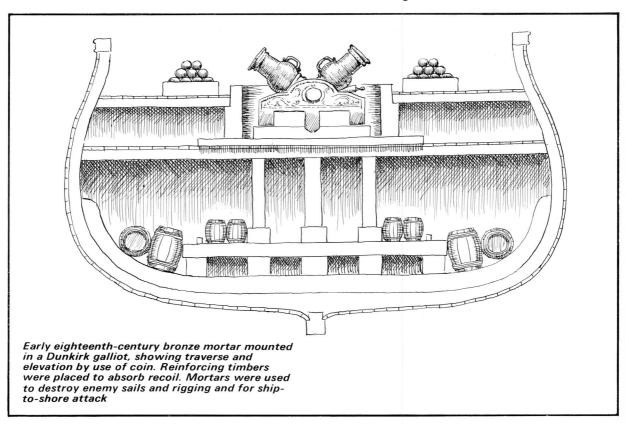

Early eighteenth-century bronze mortar mounted in a Dunkirk galliot, showing traverse and elevation by use of coin. Reinforcing timbers were placed to absorb recoil. Mortars were used to destroy enemy sails and rigging and for ship-to-shore attack

in 1695, René Duguay-Trouin had reason to be in high spirits. A year had passed since his dramatic escape from Plymouth, an incident which he recalled with amusement. If the English were to lay hands on him again, he reflected, he would be lucky to get away alive a second time. All in all, the past year had been a rewarding one. It gave him special satisfaction, for example, to think that his new flagship was the very same English warship, the *Nonsuch*, that had captured Jean Bart and Claude de Forbin and carried them to an English prison. Her name had been changed, and she had been entirely refitted after he had forced her to surrender in a battle off the south coast of England. It had been the proudest moment of his life when King Louis XIV had awarded him a sword of honour for the victory.

On his first voyage in the *Sans Pareil*, he had brought off a clever trick. Acting on information that three Dutch merchant ships were lying in the Spanish harbour of Vigo awaiting an escort vessel, Duguay-Trouin sailed boldly into port with the English Union Jack fluttering from the mast. The captains of two of the Dutch ships, recognizing the flag and the familiar outlines of an English warship and assuming that this was the escort they had been expecting, immediately weighed anchor and sailed confidently out to sea in the wake of the *Sans Pareil*. Once out of sight of Vigo, Duguay-Trouin sent a small contingent of officers and men aboard each vessel. It was only when they were addressed abruptly in French rather than English, that the Dutch captains realized they had been fooled.

Duguay-Trouin was not so lucky a couple of days later. Bound for Brest

A younger brother leads the way

with his two prizes in tow, he ran into a powerful squadron of English warships. The captain of one of the frigates was more alert and suspicious than the Dutchmen had been and directly challenged the *Sans Pareil*. Seeing no point in keeping up the deception, Duguay-Trouin raised the French flag and prepared his men for battle. Crashing broadsides from the *Sans Pareil's* forty-two cannon had soon damaged the English frigate so badly that she hoisted her red distress signal; and as two sister ships changed course to lend her assistance, Duguay-Trouin prudently slipped away under cover of darkness, bringing his prizes safely into a friendly port.

Now he was bound south once more for Spanish waters. He felt particular pride in the fact that the small frigate accompanying him, the *Léonore*, was commanded by his nineteen-year-old

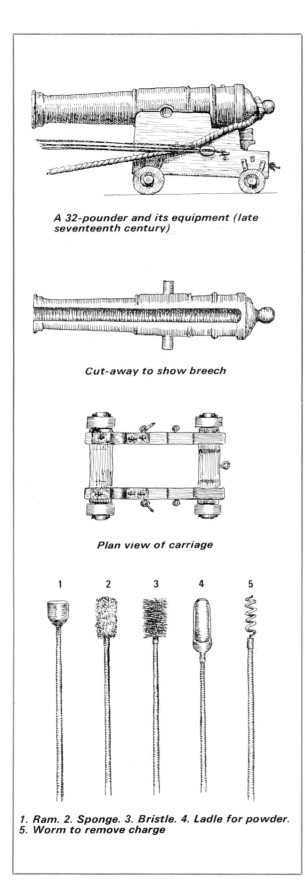

A 32-pounder and its equipment (late seventeenth century)

Cut-away to show breech

Plan view of carriage

1. Ram. 2. Sponge. 3. Bristle. 4. Ladle for powder. 5. Worm to remove charge

younger brother Etienne. Disappointingly, they had not so far sighted any enemy ships; but, at the moment, Duguay-Trouin had other problems. His supplies were running dangerously low and the most urgent priority was to find fresh water. Scanning the shore, he fixed his attention on a creek, flanked on either side by mountains. Reasoning that the river must be fed by mountain streams, René ordered the ship's launch to be lowered and was the first to climb in. Joined by Etienne and ten volunteers, he cautiously steered the boat upstream. Suddenly shots rang out from the bank. René cursed himself. They had sailed straight into a Spanish ambush.

Common sense and experience should have persuaded René to turn about and make a dash for safety. But the over-eager Etienne was already splashing ashore, yelling for the others to follow him. Instinctively, René drew his sword and leapt from the launch, hot on his brother's heels. Taken completely by surprise, the Spanish soldiers put up token resistance, then made off along the rough track running beside the river. The sound of firing had brought French reinforcements from the *Sans Pareil* onto the scene, eager to join the fray. René hesitated. Dare he risk his men in pursuing the Spaniards? Once more he allowed himself to be persuaded by Etienne. The impetuous young man had tasted battle and was in no mood to retreat. The enemy must be stationed in a nearby town or village, Etienne reasoned. One hundred and fifty armed Frenchmen would surely be more than a match for the Spanish garrison.

Reconnaissance proved Etienne correct. There was indeed a village and

there was access by footpaths both from the front and the rear. René split his force, giving his younger brother command of one group, and launched a two-pronged attack. After an hour's bitter hand-to-hand fighting, the village was captured and, having loaded themselves with arms and much-needed provisions, the French returned, flushed with success, to the ships. Their casualties had been light, but for René Duguay-Trouin the day was tinged with sadness. During the battle, Etienne had been badly wounded. Although brought safely back to the *Sans Pareil*, his condition steadily worsened and, as darkness fell, he died in his brother's arms. None of the later triumphs of a distinguished seafaring career could console René for Etienne's

death, nor sweep away the guilt he felt for his own fatal error of judgment.

The battle of Ushant

Ninety miles of open sea lie between Lizard Point, the extreme southern tip of England, and the rocky island of Ushant off the coast of Brittany, which lies farther west than any other part of French territory. It was in these waters that a great naval battle was fought in 1707 between French and English warships. On receiving reports that an English fleet was cruising southwards to Portugal, two squadrons were despatched to intercept it. Commanding them were René Duguay-Trouin and Claude de Forbin.

Duguay-Trouin had covered himself with glory in the past six years of sea warfare against England and the Netherlands; and, at the age of thirty-four he was now no common privateer but one of the most experienced captains in the French navy. The King had made him Chevalier of the Order of St Louis for his services, and his present squadron consisted of six warships. He had met Forbin for the first time only a few months previously. Well aware of the latter's reputation, he hoped fervently, as the French ships prepared for battle, that Forbin would display the nobler side of his nature in the vital hours to come.

Shortly after dawn, a convoy was sighted on the horizon. Duguay-Trouin estimated that there were more than one hundred merchantmen, escorted by several warships. His own squadron was lying astern of Forbin's ships, and it was essential to overtake them as rapidly as possible in order to plan a common course of action. When his own flagship *Le Lys* had cut down the distance between the two squadrons to a couple of miles, however, Duguay-Trouin received his first taste of his colleague's wayward behaviour. For no

apparent reason, the *Mars*, Forbin's flagship, suddenly altered course to port and was promptly followed by the other vessels under his command. This was enough to betray his identity to the commander of the English convoy. As Forbin's ships removed themselves to a safe distance, Duguay-Trouin found his own squadron exposed to the full fire-power of five enemy men-of-war, now drawn up in battle array.

Realizing that Forbin could not be counted upon to take part in the impending battle, Duguay-Trouin assembled his own ships and directed each one to attack an English warship. He was confident that his four largest ships were a match for four of the English vessels but the fifth, the *Devonshire*, posed a problem. It was a powerful ninety-gunner, against which Duguay-Trouin could only earmark the thirty-six-gun *La Gloire*. He decided not to challenge the *Devonshire* but to use *La Gloire* as a reinforcement for *Le Lys* against the English flagship, the *Cumberland*.

The battle went better than he had dared to hope. The *Cumberland*, out-

Duguay-Trouin bombards Rio de Janeiro

gunned by the two French vessels, soon hoisted the white flag. Two more English warships also surrendered and were boarded, while the third, as yet undamaged, made an escape bid. The *Devonshire*, to Duguay-Trouin's relief, had not entered the fray, and now he had the time and the necessary ships to deal with her. At this point, however, Forbin reappeared with his squadron and sailed into action against the *Devonshire*, all guns blazing. Within minutes there had been several direct hits and, before Duguay-Trouin could get within range, the English warship had caught fire. The flames spread from stem to stern and Duguay-Trouin could only watch, helplessly and horrified, as she went down with her entire crew of nine hundred men. The battle of Ushant was over.

True to form, Claude de Forbin was first with the news of the victory, arriving in Brest with his own undamaged vessels and three captured English warships, loudly proclaiming the leading role he had played in the battle. When Duguay-Trouin limped into port with his battered frigates, the celebrations were already over. All that remained was for him to present his own version of the recent naval engagement. And although King Louis never publicly committed himself, it was significant that Duguay-Trouin and not Forbin was finally promoted and rewarded.

The capture of Rio de Janeiro

In September 1711, the citizens of the Brazilian town of Rio de Janeiro awoke one night to the fury of a tropical storm. They were well accustomed to sudden torrential downpours, but on this occasion they sensed that something was different. Between the claps of thunder,

The French loot Rio

they could hear distant booming, which seemed to come from the harbour. At intervals, the sky blazed bright with flashes that were certainly not forks of lightning. And now and then there would be a much louder explosion closer to hand. Terrified and puzzled, the people of Rio anxiously awaited the dawn. As the thunder died away, shortly before first light, the explosions also ceased, to be followed by an ominous silence.

The Portuguese governor of Rio de Janeiro had also spent a sleepless night; but he at least knew exactly what was happening. The town was being bombarded by the guns of fourteen French warships lying at the entrance to the harbour. The commander of the French fleet was clearly determined to carry out his threat. Hurriedly, he issued orders for all garrisons in and around the city to prepare for an imminent land attack.

René Duguay-Trouin had looked forward to this moment. After a three-month crossing of the Atlantic the stage was set for a devastating blow at the heart of Portugal's colonial empire in the New World. A successful attack on Rio would make up for a previous French raid which had ended in disaster and would repay the Portuguese for the cold-blooded way in which they had treated their prisoners.

The expedition had been planned and organized by the French government and should have been launched in strict secrecy. But the Portuguese authorities had received prior warning of the intended raid from English spies in Brest. As soon as the French fleet came within range, Portuguese guns opened fire, causing heavy damage and casualties. Retreating to a safe distance, Duguay-Trouin sent an ultimatum to the governor, accusing him of torturing and starving the French prisoners taken in the recent attack on the town, and threatening to reduce the port to rubble if he did not surrender immediately. The governor return-

ed a spirited reply, denying the allegations of cruelty, and pledging himself to defend Rio to the last man.

Fortunately for the French, the governor's brave words hardly squared with his actions. The shattering night bombardment had the desired effect, for, by the morning, the regular soldiers manning the guns on either side of the bay were reported to have deserted their posts, leaving the town undefended. Duguay-Trouin found himself in occupation of a deserted city.

Like so many privateer captains before him, René Duguay-Trouin was unable to control his men, who ran riot through the town, looting shops and mansions in a frenzy of greed and violence. The Portuguese governor was warned that, unless he paid a heavy ransom, Rio would be burned to the ground. Playing for time, he offered to pay the sum demanded by the French in instalments, over a two-week period. Realizing that reinforcements were massing for a counter-attack, Dugunay-Trouin agreed, but took hostages to ensure that Portuguese did not go back on their word. Holding his soldiers at the ready, he was relieved to learn that the ransom had indeed been paid. Now he kept his side of the bargain and sailed for home. Although his losses had been heavy, honour had been satisfied.

'Don't move, captain'

CHAPTER FIVE

The pirates of Madagascar

It was in the early hours of the morning that Captain Gibson, master of the forty-six-gun English privateer *Charles the Second* awoke to a confused hubbub of angry voices. His head still ached from the drunken revels of the previous night, and in the flickering lamplight the faces of the men crowding around his bunk were blurred. Groaning, he propped himself on an elbow and groped for his pistol. It was gone. Rough hands pushed him down, pinned his arms, held him helpless. A head bent down, whispering fiercely in his ear. 'Don't move, captain. Nice and quiet now and you'll not be hurt!'

There was a sour stench of rum on the man's breath, and he jerked his head away, trying to focus on the black shapes milling about him.

'We've had enough, captain, understand?' came the soft menacing voice of his tormentor. 'Up with you now!'

Sudden shock gave way to rising terror. 'No, no,' he croaked feebly as he was dragged to his feet. His lips were parched, his head splitting with pain. The words, when they came, carried little conviction. 'Stop! Leave me alone! This is mutiny, do you hear, mutiny!'

His protest was greeted with mocking hoots of derision. 'Do you hear that, Long Ben?' one man shouted. 'The captain here says it's mutiny!'

The answering roar of laughter was anything but good-natured. Then there was sudden silence as the man addressed as Long Ben elbowed his way through the jostling mob. Dimly Captain Gibson made out the face of his first mate Avery. When he had first welcomed him aboard he had been amused at the joking nickname, for Long Ben was on the short, stout side. But this was not the time for joking. The man's normally placid features were stern as he faced his dazed, befuddled captain, and there was quiet authority in his voice. 'No mutiny,

The death of Thomas Tew

captain,' he murmured, 'just a change of plans. We're tired of all your promises. The men haven't been paid for eight months and there's precious little chance of taking a Frenchman at this rate. So we're off to try our fortunes in the Red Sea. Join us if you like. Otherwise be damned to you!'

Although quaking with fear, Gibson's reply was measured and firm.

'So it's pirates you aim to be, is it? Fools! I'll not go on the account with you. Do what you like with me.' A look of annoyance crossed Avery's face.

'You hear him, men,' he roared. 'Are you with him or with me?' The answering shouts left no room for doubts.

'Right,' he continued. 'Captain, we'll put you ashore here with anyone who wants to stick by you. From now on this ship's name is the *Fancy* and the men here have made me captain!' He allowed himself a brief, almost pitying smile. 'It's you who are the fool,' he said softly.

Terror in the Red Sea

It was the summer of 1695. A year had passed since the bloodless mutiny in the Spanish port of Corunna, which had transformed the privateer *Charles the Second* into the pirate ship *Fancy*. The man known variously as John Avery or Henry Every had no regrets. War against the French was not a way of getting rich and he had no intentions of heading back to the West Indies. Caribbean waters were too well patrolled nowadays, the risks too great and the rewards too small. Wealth lay farther east. From their new bases on the island of Madagascar, off the southeast coast of Africa, pirates could now cruise out into the Indian Ocean to waylay Dutch and English merchant vessels, returning to Europe with valuable cargoes from the East Indies; alternatively, they could sail north into the Gulf of Aden, ready to pounce on Moorish ships bound from the Red Sea ports of Jeddah and Mocha to Surat, some 150 miles north of Bombay. These well-armed trading vessels were in fact Indian, but the pirates used the term 'Moor' loosely to describe anyone of Moslem faith. John Avery now planned to intercept a Moorish fleet at the narrow entrance to the Red Sea.

There were three other pirate ships in addition to the *Fancy*. One of them was the *Amity*, commanded by the celebrated pirate captain Thomas Tew, whose career had followed a parallel course to that of Avery himself. Tew came from Newport, Rhode Island and boasted of once having been wined and dined by Governor Fletcher of New York, who had the reputation of taking bribes from many of the leading smugglers and pirates of the day. Tew, like Avery, had started life as a privateer and then turned pirate. His first engagement in the Red Sea was highly encouraging. After capturing a heavily armed Moorish ship, without suffering any casualties, Tew shared out plunder said to be worth £3,000 to each of his crew members.

Thomas Tew's luck did not last long. Despite the pirate blockade, most of the ships in the Moorish fleet slipped undetected through the channel by night, leaving only two to be engaged by the *Amity* and the *Fancy*. The *Fateh Mohamed* put up a strong resistance against *Amity*, and in the course of the battle Captain Tew was killed.

The most informative version of the lives and adventures of Tew, Avery and colourful contemporaries such as Kidd, Blackbeard and Roberts, is to be found

Corsair figurehead

Figurehead of Bellona, Roman goddess of war

in a book, published in 1724, entitled *A General History of the Robberies and Murders of the Most Notorious Pirates*. The author was Captain Charles Johnson, a name which some people believe may have disguised the true identity of the journalist and novelist Daniel Defoe. Whoever he was, Johnson had a flair for blood-curdling narrative. Here is his account of Tew's death. 'In the engagement a shot carried away the rim of Tew's belly, who held his bowels with his hands some small space. When he dropped, it struck such terror in his men that they suffered themselves to be taken without making resistance.' The *Amity* simply abandoned the fight, leaving Avery in the *Fancy* to finish off the *Fateh Mohamed*.

Now Avery set off in pursuit of the larger Moorish vessel, the *Gung-i-Sawai* (or, in its simplified English form, the *Gunsway*). Much larger than the *Fancy*, the *Gunsway* carried sixty-two cannon and was manned by four hundred Indian musketeers and other soldiers armed with scimitars. In addition there were hundreds of passengers, including some noblewomen returning from a pilgrimage to Mecca.

The first broadside from the *Gunsway* caught Avery unprepared and killed twenty of his men. But in the two-hour gun duel that followed, accurate firing from the *Fancy* caused heavy casualties and damage to the *Gunsway*. As Avery closed in to board the larger vessel, panic broke out among passengers and crew. With cutlasses gleaming in the sun, the English pirates swarmed on to the deck of the *Gunsway*, only to find that almost every Indian soldier had joined their captain in seeking safety in the hold. An Indian historian blamed the master of the *Gunsway* for not putting up a better fight. Had the Indians made proper use of their scimitars, he argued, the English pirates would have been repelled. Yet instead of setting an example to his men and leading them into the fray, the cowardly captain had herded on deck a terrified group of Turkish girls, placed turbans on their heads and urged them to fight a rearguard action while he and his soldiers skulked below decks!

The Pirates' Articles relating to treatment of prisoners were tossed aside by Avery's men that afternoon. All through the night they ran berserk

92

in an orgy of greed, lust and destruction. Eye-witnesses who survived the slaughter would never forget the horrors of that fateful day – the bloodstained corpses of men and women littering the deck, the groans of the dying, the screams of tortured passengers forced to hand over every last coin and piece of jewellery, the weeping of young girls brutally assaulted, and the drunken bellowing of the pirates as they ransacked the ship from stem to stern.

News of the *Gunsway* episode was greeted by furious protests in India. An elderly female relative of the Great Mogul himself had been ill-treated by the pirates, hundreds of innocent people had been killed and treasure reported to be worth £300,000* had been taken. The trading posts of the East India Company were threatened and soon both the Company and the English government were offering rewards for the capture of John Avery.

*Here, as on other occasions, estimates are very approximate. The pirates themselves tended to play down the takings.

Wreck of the Fancy

The not-so-successful pirate

In 1712 audiences in Drury Lane Theatre in London were much entertained by a play called *The Successful Pirate*, written by the mysterious Charles Johnson. The hero was obviously modelled on John Avery, but the play had a happy ending, which certainly does not square with the known facts of Avery's later career.

After his capture of the *Gunsway*, which must have brought him considerable wealth, if only for a short time, Avery was rumoured to be living in high style on Madagascar; but it was off the Bahamas that the *Fancy* next appeared. Hoping to find the governor sympathetic, Avery offered a generous bribe in return for anchorage. The governor took Avery's money but before the *Fancy* could put into port she was wrecked on a reef by a gale. Avery's luck had changed. From then on he was to be a fugitive from justice. Other

pirates who had obediently surrendered received the promised Royal Pardon, but Avery was a wanted man. The governor of Jamaica was approached, but refused to cooperate. The original crew of the *Fancy* had now split up. Avery decided to go back home and perhaps make a fresh start. He bought a sloop and sailed for Ireland with twenty men, took another ship to England and promptly vanished.

Whatever happened to Avery, he never resumed his career of piracy. Two of his former crew members received a pardon for turning King's evidence, and their information led to the trial of twenty-four pirates in October 1696. Six were hanged and the rest transported to the colony of Virginia.

John Avery was not in the dock that day and was, in fact, never found. According to the imaginative Charles Johnson, he travelled around the country under various assumed names, trying to keep going from day to day by selling what was left of the plunder he had collected. Finally some unscrupulous merchants in Bristol swindled him of his remaining diamonds by threatening to hand him over to the authorities. Betrayal would certainly have led to the gallows, for his name did not appear on the amnesty list which appeared in 1698. For a few years he lived, unrecognized and forgotten, in the north Devon port of Bideford; and it was there that, in Johnson's words, John Avery 'fell sick and died, not being worth as much as would buy him a coffin.'

Captain Kidd: the reluctant pirate

'William Kidd! You stand here charged with the deliberate murder of William Moore, gunner of the *Adventure Galley*, and with the unlawful and piratical seizure of the *Quedagh Merchant* . . . How do you plead?'

There was a long silence in the courtroom as all eyes turned towards the lonely figure of the man in the dock. Gripping the rail tightly, William Kidd looked up to face the judge. In a low voice he said, 'Not guilty, my Lord.'

It was difficult to believe that this was the man hailed as the most blood-thirsty and notorious pirate captain of the age. The press had built up a lurid picture of Captain William Kidd, but the spectators felt cheated. There was no trace here of the swaggering, boldly defiant, vicious-looking villain they had expected to see. The defendant was a plainly dressed, middle-aged man, respectable enough to be one of their neighbours. The strain of a year's confinement in Newgate Prison showed on his face. His skin was sallow, his forehead deeply lined, his eyes dull and dispirited. He peered around the court with an air of puzzled disbelief, a pathetic, isolated figure, encircled by hostile faces. For there would be no sympathy here in the Old Bailey. Captain Kidd was on trial for his life, and the evidence against him was damning.

How did a fifty-five year-old sea captain, once a respected and law-abiding citizen of New York, come to be standing trial on charges of murder and piracy, either of which carried the death penalty? Was he, as one author later wrote, ' . . . a worthy, honest-hearted, steadfast, much-enduring sailor'? Or, as another commentator put it, more bluntly, ' . . . a third-rate pirate and a fourth-rate gentleman'? Centuries after his death, nobody can say whether Captain Kidd was a reckless, brutal pirate or an irresolute,

94

indecisive privateer – the victim of his own rash temper, cruel luck and false friends.

William Kidd was born in Greenock, Scotland in 1645, served with the Royal Navy in the Dutch Wars and later settled in New York, where he married a wealthy wife and lived in comfort. The sea was his livelihood, and when England and France went to war in 1689 Kidd became a privateer. Commanding a captured French ship, which he renamed the *Blessed William* in honour of William of Orange, now on the English throne, Kidd routed a fleet of French privateers off the island of Antigua. But while the *Blessed William* was being repaired on Antigua, the crew, led by Robert Culliford, mutinied and sailed off to become pirates. Kidd was powerless to prevent his ship being stolen. For the time being, at any rate, he had no plans to turn pirate. Soon he received another command and resumed his distinguished career.

'Our trusty and well-beloved Captain Kidd'

Kidd was honoured and rewarded for further privateering exploits against the French, but in 1695 the government had concluded that the main threat to overseas trade and English shipping was now coming from English and American pirates, operating from bases in the Indian Ocean and along the coast of New England. Although English warships could not be spared to combat the pirate menace the government was prepared to finance a private venture, provided, of course, it all remained unofficial. It would be politically damaging and most embarrassing if it became known that the King himself expected to receive ten per cent of the takings, and that other backers included such eminent members of the Whig government as the First Lord of the Admiralty, the Master of the Ordnance and the Keeper of the Great Seal.

It was an old friend, Colonel Robert Livingston, who first conceived the idea of recommending William Kidd for the command of this expedition. Livingston introduced Kidd to the newly appointed Governor of New York, Lord Bellomont, who in turn proposed Kidd's name to the King. But William Kidd had good reason to be somewhat confused when he found himself in possession of two commissions from London. The first, addressed to 'our trusty and well-beloved Captain Kidd', was a standard wartime directive to attack all French shipping; but the second, which reached him seven months later, authorized him to seize the ships and persons of any pirates he might meet. Among the list of such wanted men were Thomas Tew, the drinking companion of the former Governor of New York. The names of the promoters of the venture were not revealed to Kidd, apart from Lord Bellomont who would be entitled to sixty per cent of the profits. The King would take his ten per cent and the

The press-gang at work

rest was to be shared between Livingston, Kidd and his crew. Since it was clearly understood that this would be a 'no purchase, no pay' expedition, any profit would obviously have to be in the form of plunder.

Kidd took command of his new ship, the *Adventure Galley*, early in 1696. But bad luck dogged the new venture from the start. Before Kidd even left Deptford, the press gang had removed half of his crew and he was compelled to make up the numbers in New York. On September 6, 1696, after much delay, the *Adventure Galley* at last sailed for Madagascar on its ill-fated voyage.

From privateer to pirate

A year later Kidd's *Adventure Galley* was off the Malabar Coast of India and his crew were in an ugly mood. So far it had been a tedious and unprofitable voyage. Neither in the waters around Madagascar nor during the long haul across the Indian Ocean had Kidd been able to take a prize. The ship was badly in need of repair, provisions were running dangerously low, cholera had killed forty men in one week alone and at the last port of call another twenty crew members had simply walked off and not returned.

What the more militant members of the crew particularly resented was that their captain seemed to be unable to make up his mind. In the last couple of days there had been two splendid chances of plunder, one a large East Indiaman bound for New York, another a bulky Dutch vessel. Kidd had changed course as if to attack, but on both occasions had veered away, muttering a lame excuse that the ships were too strongly armed.

Kidd could not fail to be aware of the mounting tension. The men grumbled

The killing of gunner Moore

as they half-heartedly performed their shipboard duties. Some deliberately turned their backs when Kidd approached them. There were whispers and rude sniggers as he passed. It would be only a short step from sullen disobedience to mutiny.

On the morning of October 30, 1697 Kidd was pacing the deck when he heard a sudden movement behind him. Spinning around, he saw the gunner, William Moore, with a chisel in his hand. Startled by what appeared to be a menacing gesture, Kidd's self-control snapped. Furiously, he accused Moore of being one of the leading agitators among the crew. The gunner hotly denied this but taunted Kidd for being chicken-hearted. 'That East Indiaman could have been taken without any trouble,' he countered, 'and at least we should have seen some money for our pains.' Kidd was by now on the verge of hysteria.

'You're a lousy dog,' he spluttered. Moore stood his ground and replied insolently, 'If I am, it's you who have made me one!'

It was more than Kidd could bear. Stooping, he grabbed for a heavy, iron-hooped wooden bucket and brought it crashing down on Moore's head. There was an appalled silence as he slumped to the deck. As if in a daze, Kidd ordered him to be taken below, and he turned away. Next day William Moore died of a fractured skull.

The fatal incident on the deck of the *Adventure Galley* seemed to make up Kidd's mind, for, from that day on he sprang into action, attacking and plundering small ships of many nations and allegedly torturing prisoners. Worse still, he was accused by the Indian authorities of carrying out terror raids

'Sail ho!'

on native villages in the Laccadive Islands, off the south-west coast of India, and slaughtering dozens of men, women and children. There is no way of knowing, however, whether or not these atrocities ever occurred.

It was in January 1698 that Captain Kidd had his first major success when he captured the *Quedagh Merchant*, a four hundred-ton Armenian vessel commanded by an Englishman. The valuable cargo consisted of gold, silver, jewellery and silks, and the proceeds were divided among the crew a few months later when Kidd sailed into the harbour of St Mary's Island, the famous pirate base on Madagascar. Kidd had both the *Quedagh Merchant* and another Armenian prize, the *Maiden*, in tow. The latter was set on fire and destroyed, and so too was the *Adventure Galley*, leaking so badly as to be beyond repair. The *Quedagh Merchant* now became Kidd's new flagship.

A few days after Kidd reached Madagascar, his old adversary Robert Culliford sailed into the harbour in the *Mocha*. After some initial embarrassment, the two men were soon exchanging anecdotes and drinking each other's health. But even after sharing out the loot, Kidd could not rely on the loyalty of his crew. Many of them left him to join Culliford and some of them were later brought to trial and hanged. By a further stroke of irony, Culliford himself stood in the dock with Kidd, as an accused pirate, at the Old Bailey, three years later. Culliford, with a much blacker record, was reprieved.

William Kidd now headed for home; in the West Indies he was amazed to learn that he was wanted for piracy in London.

Path to the gallows

William Kidd was confident that when he explained to his friend and patron Lord Bellomont what had really happened on the *Adventure Galley* he would be proved innocent and pardoned. To show that he had faithfully carried out his instructions, he planned to produce two French passes that he had taken from the captains of the *Quedagh Merchant* and the *Maiden*. These were documents issued by the French government protecting merchant ships from privateers. Kidd maintained that they proved conclusively that the ships were French, not Armenian, and that since England and France had been at war they were legal prizes.

Kidd's crew members were not prepared to take the risk. The bulk of them had deserted him at Madagascar and eighteen more stayed behind in the West Indies. Nor were Kidd's actions those of a man who had nothing to conceal or fear. He left the *Quedagh Merchant* in Hispaniola, transferring most of his booty to the *Antonio*, a sloop purchased from a local trader. His next port of call was on the American mainland, at Lewes, in Delaware Bay. Here more of his men went ashore with their share of the loot, promptly scattering to escape the clutches of the law. Kidd continued north to Long Island, putting in at Oyster Bay. There he wrote a letter to a famous lawyer, James Emmot, asking him to visit Lord Bellomont and to speak on his behalf. With the letter he enclosed the two French passes. Emmot duly called on Bellomont, handed over the passes and brought back an encouraging reply. If Kidd could produce his plunder and submit proof that he had not committed acts of piracy, he had nothing to worry about. 'If your case is as clear as you say,' wrote Bellomont, ' . . . I have no doubt that a King's Pardon can be obtained for you and your loyal men.'

If Kidd trusted Lord Bellomont's word he was foolish to do so. All the colonial governors had strict orders to apprehend Kidd and his accomplices. The war with France was over and Bellomont was in deadly earnest in pursuing his campaign to stamp out piracy. Consequently he was quite prepared to disown the man he had himself employed as a privateer.

Whether or not Kidd believed Bellomont's promise, he took pains to dispose of most of his remaining plunder before sailing the *Antonio* back to Boston. At Gardiner's Island, off the tip of Long Island, he landed a number of chests and bales, and also transferred some cargo into sloops bound for New York. He made a further halt at

Captain Kidd flung into a Boston gaol

Block Island, where he was joined by his wife and children. From here he seems to have made a further attempt to smooth relations with his former patron by despatching to Lady Bellomont four diamonds and two rings – gifts that were not accepted. On July 2, 1699 he stepped ashore at Boston. A couple of days later Bellomont had him arrested. He was thrown into prison, and bound hand and foot with heavy iron shackles.

The following spring William Kidd was shipped home to England for trial. But he languished in Newgate for another thirteen months before appearing for the first time in the dock at the Old Bailey. By that time the affair had been blown up into a national scandal. The prominent members of the Whig government were desperate to clear themselves of charges of having financed a pirate expedition; and the jubilant Tory opposition, together with most of the Press, were determined to see Captain Kidd hanged. By the time the trial began, Lord Bellomont was dead, having gone on record as proclaiming, 'There was never a greater liar or thief in the world than this Kidd.'

The treasure that never was

It was Captain Kidd's mysterious activities on Gardiner's Island which sparked off the first rumours of buried

Some pirate flags. (Top to bottom) *French filibusters, Bartholomew Roberts, Stede Bonnet*

Merchant, he was undoubtedly exaggerating. In any case the ship was by then a burnt-out hulk. Whatever he had left aboard had long since been sold or pilfered by his men. As for the 'treasure' he took ashore at Gardiner's Island, this apparently consisted of several bales and chests, of which one, according to John Gardiner who owned the island, contained gold and possibly silver. But Lord Bellomont lost no time in retrieving this treasure as well as bits and pieces from other places. It was all sent to London and listed. There were 1,111 ounces of gold, in the form of dust and bars, and 2,353 ounces of silver, estimated to be worth about £14,000. And after his death his personal valuables were auctioned for approximately £6,450. Evidently Captain Kidd had not been destitute, but he was far from being a millionaire.

'The innocentest person of them all'

On May 8, 1701 Captain Kidd appeared before six judges at the Old Bailey on charges of murder and piracy. There were, in fact, four separate trials, lasting two days, and six indictments. The first charge was the murder of his gunner William Moore; the second and third accused him of the illegal seizure of the *Quedagh Merchant* and the *Maiden*; the other three were minor cases of piracy and looting.

The cards were stacked against Kidd from the start. The court had virtually made up its mind to find him guilty, and the public was howling for his blood. Under the rules of the day he had to undertake his own defence, and since the only members of his crew who could support his version of events were in the dock with him on piracy charges he was not allowed to call them as wit-

treasure worth millions of pounds. The myth of Kidd's treasure hoard gathered momentum during the two and a half centuries following his death, and as recently as 1951 expeditions were mounted to recover the vast wealth that the pirate was alleged to have concealed before he was brought to justice. Although treasure-seekers of the future are unlikely to be deterred, there is not a scrap of evidence that this secret cache ever existed.

It would seem certain that by the time Kidd brought the *Antonio* into Boston harbour most of his own share of any plunder had dwindled away. Although he boasted to Lord Bellomont of the value of the cargo on the *Quedagh*

nesses. The only two prosecution witnesses were also former crew members, but both had deserted in Madagascar and had been promised a pardon if they turned King's evidence. They duly stood up in court and provided enough damning evidence against Kidd to make the verdict a foregone conclusion.

As the judges rapped out question after question, Kidd became increasingly confused. His answers were often rambling and evasive. Sometimes he contradicted himself. But on the main issues he was quite positive, and he firmly denied both the murder and the piracy charges.

As the hours dragged on, the questions became more and more hostile and Kidd's replies almost desperate.

'You admit striking gunner Moore with a bucket?'

'Yes, but he provoked me. He was planning a mutiny.'

'But the witnesses here – members of your crew – deny he was a mutineer. They say you attacked him and that the force of the blow killed him.'

'Not true, my Lord. He was a sick man. The blow was not powerful enough to have caused his death.'

'You lie, William Kidd! One of the prosecution witnesses was your ship's surgeon. He tended gunner Moore from the moment of the incident to the time he died. He has testified that there can be no doubt as to the cause of death . . . We find you guilty!'

Kidd fared no better on the piracy charges.

'You do not deny taking these vessels?'

'No, but there was no question of piracy. I was acting within my rights as a privateer.'

'We suggest that you deliberately and repeatedly committed acts of piracy, including looting and the incitement of your crew to rape, torture and the slaughter of innocent men, women and children!'

'If this was so, my Lord, it was they who urged me against my will. I was

Kidd on trial at the Old Bailey

A grim warning

unable to check their base desires.'

'What about these two French passes you say you took from the captains of the *Quedagh Merchant* and the *Maiden*?'

'I handed them to Mr Emmot and charged him to give them to Lord Bellomont. I cannot say . . . '

'Then where are they, Mr Kidd?'

'My Lord, I swear to you they were in my possession. They proved . . . '

'Come now, Sir, you cannot expect us to believe this . . . And why, if these vessels were legitimate prizes as you allege, did you not bring them back to New York for the matter to be judged?'

'My Lord, I had a mutiny on my hands. I was forced to share out the plunder at Madagascar. Then the ships became unseaworthy and we burned them.'

'Where are the log-books providing a true and detailed account of the voyage of the *Adventure Galley*?'

'When my crew mutinied, my Lord, they took the log books with them.'

'Indeed, Sir, how very convenient! Have you no more convincing proof than this? No? Then we shall retire to consider our verdict.' It took the panel of judges only ten minutes. 'William Kidd, we find you guilty on all charges and hereby sentence you to be hanged and your body suspended in chains. Have you anything further to say?' The prisoner looked up, shook his head as if unable to believe his ears. 'My Lord,' he stammered, 'it is a very hard sentence. For my part, I am the innocentest person of them all.'

On May 23, 1701 William Kidd was driven in a cart to Execution Dock at Wapping and hanged in front of a rowdy, exuberant crowd. Even at that critical stage his luck deserted him once more. The rope snapped and he had to be lifted on to the gallows again. His body was taken down-river to Tilbury, to be suspended in chains.

Lawyers have argued ever since as to whether he was guilty and whether he received a fair trial. The killing of William Moore might have been manslaughter; but at some stage Kidd must have taken the decision to turn pirate. But there is an interesting scrap of information which indicates that he was telling the truth in one respect. In 1911 the two passes which Kidd swore he had handed over came to light at the Public Records Office in London. It seems certain that they were forwarded as promised by Lord Bellomont and then deliberately concealed by the Admiralty. Innocent Kidd may not have been, but he hardly deserved his reputation.

James Plantain: King of Ranter Bay

Not all pirates who terrorized shipping in the Indian Ocean met such a dreadful end as William Kidd. Some of the adventurers who visited the beautiful tropical island of Madagascar found life so delightful that they settled there for good. One of them was the man known as the King of Ranter Bay.

When Commodore Thomas Matthews put in at the island in the course of his pirate-hunting expedition on behalf of the British government, some twenty years after the death of Captain Kidd, he had an unexpected reception. On the beach he and his landing party were challenged by an elegantly dressed white man, with a brace of pistols in his sash, accompanied by a dozen fierce-looking armed natives.

'Permit me to introduce myself,' he said politely, 'I am the King of Ranter

James Plantain of Ranter Bay

Bay. May I invite you and your men to visit my palace?'

The guns and spears levelled so menacingly in his direction left Matthews little choice. The palace turned out to be a stout fortress, but the entertainment was indeed royal. After several hours of feasting and drinking, Commodore Matthews was on the best of terms with his host. The only thing that slightly disturbed him was that he knew that his duty was to arrest the man sitting opposite and jovially toasting his health. For the King of Ranter Bay was on the wanted list – an ex-pirate named James Plantain. Furthermore, two of his most trusted 'courtiers' were also pirates, James Adair, a Scot, and Hans Burgen from Denmark. James Plantain, born in Jamaica, had done well out of piracy and was now a wealthy man. Madagascar was divided up into a number of little kingdoms, which were continually warring with one another, and Plantain had declared himself ruler of the Ranter Bay territory at the southern tip of the island. It was no empty title. He commanded a large, well-trained native army and his court offered all the luxuries expected of a local king, including a number of beautiful wives, dressed in rich silks and decked in jewellery, who were called by such improbable names as Moll, Sue and Peg.

Impressed by Plantain's warm hospitality and armed strength, Commodore Matthews prudently decided to trade with the King of Ranter Bay and then sailed home, where he was promptly relieved of his command for failing to perform his duty.

Meanwhile James Plantain continued living in regal style in his island paradise. But all was not as peaceful as it seemed. Tiring of his pretty but stupid wives, King James of Ranter Bay fell in love with the granddaughter of King Dick of Massaleage, on the west coast of Madagascar. Her name was Eleanore Brown, supposedly the daughter of an English sailor, and in addition to being beautiful she spoke a few words of English. But when Dick refused to allow the marriage, King James declared war.

The commander of the Ranter Bay forces was a powerfully built man known as Mulatto Tom, who was said to be the son of the famous pirate John Avery and the daughter of the Great Mogul – highly unlikely, but impossible to disprove. Together with allies and the forces of kings who deserted from the other side, Plantain's army consisted of several thousand troops, armed with lances and rifles. Flying their English, Scottish and Danish colours, they inflicted a crushing defeat on King Dick and his allies. And when he discovered that his bride-to-be had been having an affair with one of the English pirates who had died for King Dick, James Plantain took cruel revenge – but not on her. He executed her unfortunate grandfather and burned the town of Massaleage. After many wars against other kings, he finally took the title of King of Madagascar.

A man who wields supreme power is bound to make enemies. Generous to his friends, he was cruel to those who opposed him. When he learned of plots against his life, he decided it was time to leave his island kingdom. Taking Eleanore and their children, Plantain sailed in a sloop for the Malabar Coast of India. History does not record what happened to the King of Ranter Bay, but here was one pirate who could claim that crime did pay.

Blackbeard's joke

CHAPTER SIX

Piracy's final fling

In the cabin of the *Queen Anne's Revenge* three men sat around the table drinking, their shadows thrown across walls and low ceiling by the guttering light of a candle. The huge figure of the captain dwarfed those of his companions, the ship's mate and the sailing master. He was almost completely drunk, his voice slurred, his bloodshot eyes glinting maliciously out of the tangled black mass of hair covering his face. The men fiddled uneasily with their beer mugs, laughing obediently at his coarse jokes. In this mood he was as dangerous as a wild animal and the slightest slip of the tongue on their part might send him mad with rage. So

although they pretended to be relaxed, both men were on their guard.

It happened so suddenly that there was no time even to push their chairs back out of harm's way. One moment the big man's hands were resting flat on the table, the next they were out of sight. A split second later the candle was blown out, followed by two loud explosions as the captain let fire with a pair of pistols under the table. The scream of pain as a bullet ripped through the leg of Israel Hands, the sailing master, was drowned by a boom of triumphant laughter from the man who had fired the shot. Israel Hands was crippled for life. For Captain

Edward Teach, better known as Blackbeard, it was an amusing practical joke.

Blackbeard the terrible

The famous pirate known as Blackbeard was something of a mystery in his lifetime and the recorded facts of his career at sea span only a few years, from 1716 when his name first appeared in official documents, to 1718 when he fought his last battle. It is not known whether he was born in Bristol or in Jamaica and there is even disagreement about his real name which was variously given as Edward Teach, Tatch or Thatch. But to the men who served under him and the authorities who hunted him he was always known, for obvious reasons, as Blackbeard.

Captain Charles Johnson, who never actually met him, conjured up this vivid description of the terrible pirate who 'frightened America more than any comet'. The most distinctive fea-

The terrifying Captain Teach

ture was, of course, the black beard, 'which he suffered to grow of an extravagant length; as to breadth, it came up to his eyes. He was accustomed to twist it with ribbons, in small tails . . . and turn them about his ears. In time of action,' continued Johnson, 'he wore a sling over his shoulders, with three brace of pistols hanging in holsters like bandoliers, and stuck lighted matches under his hat, which, appearing on each side of his face, his eyes naturally looking fierce and wild, made him altogether such a figure that imagination cannot form an idea of a fury from Hell more frightful.'

Blackbeard's reputation in and around the waters of North and Central America, where he played havoc with merchant shipping was as sinister as his name and appearance, although some of the legends do strain belief. One story says that he had no less than fourteen wives who were forced to dance for him while dodging bullets that he fired at their feet. Later he enticed them one by one down to his underground vault, walling them up as they gloated over his money and jewels. Evidently someone must have confused him with that fairytale villain Bluebeard!

Nevertheless, to the captains of many ships attacked and plundered in the Caribbean Blackbeard was a real and much-hated figure. Port Royal was no longer a hotbed of piracy but the port of Nassau on New Providence, one of the islands of the Bahamas, was a good substitute. It was from this base that Blackbeard sailed in his flagship, the captured French merchantman which he had renamed the *Queen Anne's Revenge*. It was here that he built up a small but powerful fleet that preyed on shipping off the American coasts, from Virginia down to Florida; and it was in these waters that he formed a temporary alliance with another American pirate, Major Stede Bonnet.

Unequal partners

Joining forces with the notorious Blackbeard was not one of the wiser decisions of Stede Bonnet. A wealthy middle-aged planter from Barbados, he was said to have taken to piracy because of a wife who nagged him beyond endurance. Bonnet was reasonably successful at it so long as he was on his own, raiding shipping from New England southwards to Carolina in his armed sloop the *Revenge*. Blackbeard, however, was far from impressed with Bonnet's record and made it clear from the start that this was to be a partnership on his terms.

'Commanding a sloop is a tiring business,' he informed the unhappy Bonnet. 'I seriously doubt whether you have the patience and experience. Why not let my captain and trustworthy crew relieve you of the responsibility?'

And with these friendly words Blackbeard took over the *Revenge*, literally reducing the major to the ranks.

For a while Bonnet put up with the humiliation. He was certainly present on the curious occasion when Blackbeard blockaded the port of Charleston, holding a prominent member of the town council as hostage together with a number of prisoners from a captured ship bound for England. Yet with the town at his mercy all Blackbeard demanded in return was a chestful of medical supplies. Henry Morgan would hardly have allowed a besieged city to escape so lightly.

It was obvious to Stede Bonnet that

Obverse and reverse sides of a Spanish cob (or piece of eight) minted 1733

he was not going to make a fortune by taking orders from Blackbeard and he soon got his chance to recover his independence. Unpredictable as always, Blackbeard deliberately wrecked the *Queen Anne's Revenge* off the North Carolina coast, sailing off in a sloop with his most loyal crew members and a large amount of plunder which did not belong to him. Although he had been cheated of his share Bonnet was happy to see the last of Blackbeard and get back his old ship which he renamed the *Royal James*.

Stede Bonnet only had a few months to enjoy his new-found freedom for he was high on the wanted list of dangerous pirates. When Governor Johnson of South Carolina heard that the *Royal James*, badly damaged, had been sighted with two prizes at the mouth of Cape Fear River, he sent two armed sloops to capture or destroy her. In the battle which followed neither the authorities nor the pirates showed much skill in navigation, both sides running their sloops aground in the shallows. But when Bonnet realised that he was trapped and outgunned he hoisted the white flag of surrender.

Bonnet was not finished, however, and gave Governor Johnson a good run for his money. Imprisoned in a private house, as was considered fitting for a man of his background, he bribed the guards and escaped in a small boat. A reward of £700 was offered and Colonel William Rhett, who had commanded the naval operation in the Cape Fear River, had the satisfaction of tracking down Bonnet and taking him prisoner for the second time. But there was to be no more escaping. Taken in irons to Charleston, Major Stede Bonnet was tried and condemned to die with thirty of his men. He did not face execution with as much composure as William Kidd. In Charles Johnson's words, 'When his dissolution drew nigh, all his resolution failed him, and his fears and agonies so wrought upon him that he was scarce sensible when he came to the place of execution.' A pardon might have been given had he not escaped when originally arrested. As it was, ' . . . the Major's friends considered that it would be a great expense and trouble to no matter of purpose, except the lengthening out of a wretched life some small time longer . . . ' So they refused to appeal on his behalf to the King and let him hang.

The end of Blackbeard

Meanwhile the pirating days of Edward Teach were also numbered. In continuing to attack French ships off Bermuda he knew the risk he was run-

The battle of Pamlico Sound

ning. He had scornfully turned down the British government's offer of pardon to all pirates surrendering by a given date. The deadline had passed and Blackbeard could expect no mercy if and when taken.

Although many colonial governments were howling for his blood, Blackbeard counted on the firm support and protection of one man who was in his debt, Governor Charles Eden of North Carolina. Eden was virtually on Blackbeard's payroll, having allowed him to set up a secure base in Pamlico Sound. Not only was he immune from arrest in North Carolina waters but he had a guaranteed outlet in the town of Bath for his plunder and contraband – provided Eden continued to receive his generous share. On shore Blackbeard enjoyed complete freedom and Eden even graced his wedding to a sixteen-year-old girl (rumoured to be the last of his fourteen wives).

So long as he retained Governor Eden's friendship Blackbeard was un-

touchable. But as time passed there were angry reactions from local citizens to the scandalous behaviour of the pirate captain, who strutted through Bath as if he owned the town, and of his men, whose drunken brawling was a threat to lives and property. Finally a group of leading citizens appealed to Governor Alexander Spotswood of the neighbouring colony of Virginia to take the firm action which they could not expect from their own authorities. And when, in November 1718, Spotswood learned that Blackbeard had dropped anchor in the waters of Ocracoke Inlet at the entrance to Pamlico Sound, he took matters into his own hands.

Since warships could not negotiate the shallows, Spotswood fitted out two sloops to hunt for Blackbeard. Commanding the expedition was Lieutenant Robert Maynard, an officer of the Royal Navy. The fifty-five men, all naval recruits, had an added incentive to risk their lives against the notorious pirate and his crew. An official proclamation promised rich rewards for a successful action: ' . . . for Edward Teach, commonly called Captain Teach or Blackbeard, £100 for every other commander of a pirate ship, sloop or vessel, £40 for every lieutenant, master or quartermaster, boatswain or carpenter, £20; for every other inferior officer, £15, and for every private man taken aboard such ship, sloop or vessel, £10.'

Maynard sighted Blackbeard's nine-gun sloop at dusk and anchored close to shore overnight. If the pirates were aware of the navy's presence they gave no obvious signs, judging by the sounds of drunken shouts and laughter that floated across the water. At dawn Maynard's sloops closed in. Relying on his familiarity with the dangerous shoals and sandbanks, Blackbeard manoeuvred his ship towards the shore. Following him, both the naval sloops ran aground and as they were lying helpless the pirate vessel fired a broad-

Blackbeard at bay

side, killing the captain and several crew members of the smaller ship. But Maynard's seagoing experience matched Blackbeard's and by tossing heavy equipment overboard he worked his sloop free and bore down on the pirate ship. Now the tables were turned. As Blackbeard desperately tried to hoist sail he too ran aground and Maynard ordered his men to prepare for a boarding attempt.

The gap between the two ships was so narrow that Maynard could distinguish the huge figure of Blackbeard ordering his men to battle stations. When Maynard yelled across for him to surrender, the pirate captain's deep voice boomed back in defiance.

'Damn you for villains! Who are you?' 'No pirates!' replied Maynard.

'Then come aboard,' roared Blackbeard, 'and let me see who you are!'

'I will come aboard as soon as I can,' Maynard coolly answered, 'with my sloop!'

There was silence for a moment as Blackbeard sized up the situation. Then he grabbed a bowl of rum and downed it in one gulp.

'Damnation seize my soul,' he bellowed angrily, 'if I give you quarter or expect any from you!'

Maynard's reply was lost in the crash of gunfire from the pirate sloop. When the smoke cleared twenty naval ratings lay dead. Clearly Blackbeard meant business.

Maynard did some quick thinking. Ordering the survivors below he tempted Blackbeard aboard his own sloop. Seeing only the captain and the helmsman on deck, the pirates swarmed over the rails, expecting an easy prize. But as they rushed for the poop thirty sailors burst out of the hold and attacked them from the rear. Blackbeard realized, too late, that he had tumbled into his enemy's trap. In the fierce hand-to-hand fighting that followed all his men were killed or wounded, some jumping overboard to save their lives. Blackbeard was the last to fall, fighting desperately with pistol and cutlass against a dozen men lunging at him with swords from every side. He was bleeding from a score of wounds when Maynard himself mercifully delivered the accurate pistol shot that ended his life. As proof of his mission Maynard cut off the dead pirate's head and stuck it on the bowsprit, sailing back to Bath to claim his reward.

'Here was the end,' commented Charles Johnson, 'of that courageous brute, who might have passed for a hero had he been employed in a good cause.'

There is an ironic footnote to the story. Fourteen surviving members of Blackbeard's crew were tried and hanged, mainly as a result of evidence provided by one man who, in return, was granted a free pardon. That man was Israel Hands, former sailing master of the *Queen Anne's Revenge*, who had been the victim of Blackbeard's little practical joke in that darkened cabin and who now, lame and penniless, could reckon that in some measure he had evened the score.

Amazons of the high seas

Outwardly John Rackham was everything a pirate should be. Nicknamed Calico Jack because of the colourfully patterned calico shirt and trousers he wore, he was a handsome man with a weakness for strong drink and pretty girls. Having served his apprenticeship with John Avery, Calico Jack now commanded his own pirate ship, raiding shipping off the American coast and among the Caribbean islands. But Calico Jack's bright clothes and swaggering manner concealed a streak of cowardice. He would not pick a fight unless the odds were heavily in his favour and when faced with a situation demanding decisiveness and bravery he failed to show the qualities of leadership which might have won him the loyalty of his crew and the respect of his foes.

For all that, John Rackham cut a dashing figure. It was in the port of Charleston that he won the heart of a girl named Anne Bonny. Born in Ireland, the daughter of a lawyer, Anne had emigrated as a child to South Carolina. But she had tossed away her chance to inherit her father's fortune when she eloped with James Bonny, an American pirate. When her husband became a paid informer she abandoned him, falling in love with a succession of other pirates and finally running off to sea with Calico Jack. For Anne was not the sort of girl who was content to sit at home sewing, cultivating a small vegetable patch and reading the Bible. She wanted to share her lover's adventures, to show that she was as tough and as courageous as any of the men among his crew. She wanted no privileges, simply to put on pirates' clothes, carry out normal shipboard duties and be in the thick of the battle when they took a prize.

Calico Jack agreed to have her on board with some misgivings. Although with her close-cropped hair and baggy shirt she might pretend to be a man the deception could not be kept up for very long. And it was against all the rules – almost unheard of – for women to become pirates. But Anne got her way.

The men respected her because she soon proved that she could handle a rope and flourish a cutlass with the best of them; and they kept their distance when they realized she was the captain's woman.

Rackham was a jealous, quick-tempered man and he could not keep watch on her all the time. One morning he saw Anne in conversation with one of the crew. Rackham had paid no particular notice to this lad, a fairly new recruit, and he certainly did not like the way they were whispering and giggling together. This was too much! Blind with rage, he drew his cutlass and advanced on the secretive pair, grabbing the man by the elbow and flinging him to the deck.

'Stop, Jack!' shouted Anne. 'For Heaven's sake, let her alone. She means no harm!'

John Rackham lowered his cutlass. His eyes met those of the pirate at his feet. They were sparkling, mischievous eyes and they were beyond doubt those of a woman.

Calico Jack evidently had two women in his pirate crew and this new one proved to be as spirited and determined as his own Anne. Her name was Mary Read, English by birth, and with a tempestuous career as a soldier already behind her.

Disguised as a man, Mary had fought against the French, first with the infantry and then with a cavalry regiment. But her plans to become an officer were dashed when she fell madly in love with a Dutch trooper, whom she soon married. But when, after only a few months, her husband died, Mary once more surrendered to the call of adventure, trimmed her hair, donned male clothing and set sail in a Dutch ship for the West Indies. On the voyage they were attacked and captured by pirates and from that moment Mary knew that she had found a new career. By the time she joined Calico Jack she had seen plenty of action both with privateers and pirates and she struck up a close friendship with Anne Bonny.

Romance blossomed again for Mary Read when the pirates took a Jamaican merchant ship, forcing the survivors to become members of their crew. One of the reluctant recruits was a good-looking young carpenter, and the pair planned to get married.

Duel at dawn

Mary Read's husband-to-be was affable but shy. With his delicate build and refined manners he was constantly being teased. Finally the taunts and practical jokes became so cruel that he could stand it no longer and in a sudden burst of fury challenged one of the burliest, most brutal members of the crew to a duel the next day. Mary, fiercely protective, was horror-struck. Her lover

might soon be dead. What could she do?

The answer came in a flash. Nobody save Calico Jack, Anne Bonny and her future husband knew that she was a woman. All she had to do was pick a quarrel with the same pirate and provoke him into a separate duel. That evening she carried out her plan. Befuddled with drink, he did not realize that Mary had fixed the duel some hours prior to the other one.

The ship was conveniently anchored off a small island and next day, shortly after sunrise, the crew trooped ashore. On the sand by the water's edge, ten paces apart, Mary and her grinning, confident rival raised their pistols and took aim. The two shots rang out simultaneously and the big man crumpled bleeding to the ground. Without hesitation Mary drew her cutlass and ran him through.

'We plead our bellies'

Mary was no luckier in her second marriage than in her first. The Governor of

Mary Read fights a duel

Jamaica had sent out a sloop to capture John Rackham and his crew and one morning the pirate ship was found at anchor in a remote island cove. The pirates were caught unprepared. The guns were not loaded and Rackham and most of the crew were blind drunk. As the sailors clambered aboard only Anne Bonny and Mary Read put up any resistance.

A few weeks later they were all standing trial at St Jago de la Vega in Jamaica. Calico Jack behaved with no more gallantry and courage in court than he had in his last fight. Knowing that his own case was hopeless, he made sure to implicate the others; and both he and all the other male members of the crew swore that not only were Anne and Mary willing pirates but that they were more cruel and vicious than anyone else. Yet it was the women who had the last word. When all the pirates were condemned to death and the judge asked whether they had anything to say, two of them looked him boldly in the eye and announced, 'My Lord, we plead our bellies!'

Mary Read and possibly Anne Bonny as well were pregnant, and in accordance with the law both were spared. Mary did not live long for soon after being sent to prison she caught a fever and died. Anne Bonny served her sentence and was released. Nothing more is known of her. She was allowed to visit John Rackham the night before he was executed.

'I am sorry,' she said, 'to see you here. But if you had fought like a man you need not have hanged like a dog!'

Bartholomew Roberts: pirate of principle

In the summer of 1719 a fleet of forty-two

Portuguese merchant ships, escorted by two men-of-war, lay in the harbour of Bahia in Brazil, about to sail for Lisbon. Portuguese ships carrying colonial produce such as sugar, tobacco, timber and hides had been running the gauntlet of pirates in the South Atlantic for more than a century, but in recent years the stakes of this perilous game had been raised. For at long last Portuguese prospectors had discovered gold in Brazil and now the bullion was flowing back to Europe in ever-increasing quantities. For a pirate prepared to run the risk Portuguese gold was an enticing prospect. Bartholomew Roberts was not by nature a gambler. As he surveyed the Portuguese fleet from the deck of the *Royal Rover* his cool, methodical mind turned over the possibilities. One thing was certain. Having come this far he was not going to sail away empty-handed.

Bartholomew Roberts, born in Wales, had been at sea for many years when he was captured by a pirate vessel commanded by another Welshman, Howel Davis, off the African coast of Guinea. When Davies was killed in action against the Portuguese only a few weeks later Roberts was elected captain in his place for he had already impressed his shipmates with his rare combination of courage and common sense. Roberts accepted their decision with good grace, reflecting, in the words of Charles Johnson, that 'since he had dipped his hands in muddy water and must be a pirate, it was better being a commander than a common man.'

Roberts was a stern disciplinarian, making sure that his men observed ship's rules to the letter. He would allow no dicing or card-playing, lights and candles had to be put out by eight o'clock – a sensible precaution against fire – and any drinking had to take place on deck. He himself took no alcohol but he did have one personal weakness – fashionable clothes.

After taking command of the *Royal Rover* Roberts allowed the men to avenge Davis' death by burning a Portuguese fort and sinking a couple of ships but forbade them to engage in indiscriminate killing and plundering – further proof that he was a man with higher principles than many other brutal adventurers such as Thomas Tew or John Avery. Then he sailed westward to the coasts of Brazil; and after weeks of frustrating inactivity he entered the port of Bahia.

A frontal attack against dozens of well-armed enemy ships would be sheer

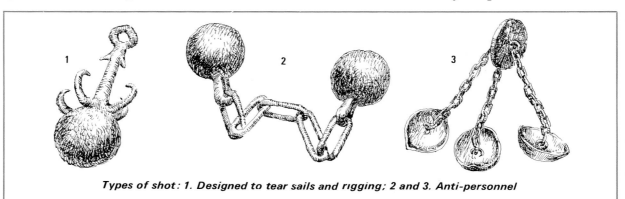

Types of shot: 1. Designed to tear sails and rigging; 2 and 3. Anti-personnel

lunacy. Ordering most of his men below he steered the *Royal Rover* boldly into the bay where the Portuguese ships were anchored. Coming abreast with one of them he cheerfully hailed the captain and beckoned him on board. Assuming that such an open approach would only be made by an ally, the Portuguese captain, unescorted, clambered up the side.

'Welcome aboard,' announced Roberts. Make no sound or sign, I beg you, and you'll come to no harm.'

The poor man had little choice.

'Now,' continued Roberts affably, 'kindly inform me which of these ships carries the most valuable cargo.'

A quivering finger pointed towards a large vessel, the *Sagrada Familia*. 'Thank you,' smiled Roberts. 'Perhaps you will join us in paying her a visit.'

So far so good. But by this time the strange ship in their midst had aroused Portuguese suspicions. As Roberts bore down on the *Sagrada Familia* the crew could be seen hurrying about the deck to their battle stations. A broadside from the *Royal Rover* sent them scurrying for shelter. Within ten minutes a British boarding party had forced the Portuguese to hand over their ship.

Bursts of cannon fire from nearby ships now sounded the alarm but by the time the two warships arrived on the scene Roberts' men had sailed the *Sagrada Familia* out to sea, closely followed by the *Royal Rover*. Roberts had amply repaid his crew. The chests of gold coins were worth a fortune.

'A merry life and a short one'

Bartholomew Roberts was too wily to try the same trick twice. The following year he was responsible for another sensational exploit, this time far to the

Bartholomew Roberts hoists his flag

north in an area seldom frequented by pirates – the coast of Newfoundland. His new flagship, the *Royal Fortune*, was a converted Rhode Island sloop mounting only ten guns and with a small crew of sixty men. His entry into Trepanny Bay was, on the face of it, as reckless as his descent on Bahia the previous year. But instead of slipping in unobserved, the *Royal Fortune* attacked to the ear-splitting accompaniment of beating drums and braying trumpets. At her masthead fluttered two flags, the British ensign and the pirate emblem of death's head and cutlass. The attack was so sudden and so brilliantly engineered that although there were some twenty-two British and French ships in the harbour not one of them fired a shot. Roberts had a field-day. Not only did he capture and ransack every vessel in the bay but he held the port and town for ten days, plundering at will. Even Governor Spotswood of Virginia, the man who had hunted down Blackbeard, paid grudging tribute to the daring of the Welsh sea captain, while vowing to bring him to justice.

By this time, Bartholomew Roberts was relishing every moment of his pirating career. From Newfoundland he sailed to the West Indies, playing havoc with peaceful shipping. He won no new friends in the process. So chilly were his receptions at the hands of the French governor of Martinique and the British governor of Barbados that he designed a new pirate flag, showing himself standing on two skulls, bearing the initials ABH (A Barbadian's Head) and AMH (A Martiniquian's Head). At St Christopher he left his visiting card in the form of sinking ships and burning buildings. News of this apparently reached the ears of the authorities on the island of St Bartholomew where the governor offered Roberts and his crew a warmer welcome, including banquets, gifts and the favours of the loveliest local girls.

After a year in the Caribbean there seemed little scope for new adventures. In only three years of piracy Roberts had set up something of a record, having captured more than four hundred ships. Now he headed back for his original field of operations – the West African coast.

Too many successes, however, led to over-confidence and he failed to notice that two British warships were patrolling these waters. What was more, they were hot on his trail. Roberts now had

116

three ships, including a captured frigate to which he had given the same name as that of his previous flag-ship, the *Royal Fortune*. All three ships were sighted on a January morning in 1722 by Captain Chaloner Ogle, commander of the *Swallow*. Assuming she was a Portuguese vessel Roberts sent the *Great Ranger*, the larger of his two escort ships, in pursuit. Ogle pretended to give ground, then rounded on the pirate ship, killing ten of the crew.

Surprisingly, this setback did not put Roberts on his guard. Only two days later Captain Ogle rounded Cape Lopez and trapped the *Royal Fortune*, lying quietly at anchor with a prize. Bartholomew Roberts was still at breakfast, enjoying a spicy dish of meat, fish and vegetables known as *salmagundi*. Many of his men were sleeping off the effects of heavy drinking from a party the night before. For once the famous pirate was caught unprepared. At a

Captain Roberts is trapped

shouted warning from above he rushed out on deck, immaculately dressed in his crimson waistcoat and trousers and his red-feathered hat. But as he bellowed for his drowsy crew to man the cannons a broadside rang out from the *Swallow* and he fell, clutching his throat. When his officers reached his side he was already dead.

The dispirited crew surrendered. Of the one hundred and sixty-nine men who stood trial, fifty-two were hanged. Ogle was knighted for his action, but he was cheated of his main prize, because Roberts who, in his own words, described piracy as 'a merry life and a short one' died as he surely would have wished – on the deck of his ship, dressed in the height of fashion.

The pirates of Barataria Bay

The coastal belt of the state of Louisiana is bayou country – a flat green wilderness of forest and swampland, criss-crossed by sluggish, weed-infested streams and rivers, dotted with lakes whose placid waters mirror the encircling trees. At the turn of the 19th century it was a forbidding yet strangely beautiful region, the haunt of alligators and water moccasins, of bears and wildcats, of wild geese, ducks, herons and a dazzling array of tropical birds. Periodically immense areas would be engulfed in the flood waters of the mighty Mississippi and its tributaries. But although steamboats would soon be plying up and down the great river, the bayou waterways were only navigable by canoe. Some of the streams snaked for miles through marsh and tall undergrowth, only to peter out or come to a dead end. Others wound and twisted their way down to the sea, flowing into the broad island-studded bays of the Gulf of Mexico. The largest of these, Barataria Bay, could be entered from the sea only by a narrow passage be-

tween two long, sandy islands, Grande Terre and Grande Île. These islands were for many years the fortified headquarters of the brothers Jean and Pierre Lafitte; and Barataria Bay with its hinterland of lakes, creeks and swamps was their undisputed domain.

Of French birth, the Lafitte brothers originally ran a blacksmith's business in nearby New Orleans but from 1807 onwards they turned their talents to smuggling, piracy and slave-trading. Barataria was an ideal base, sheltered from wind and storm, within striking distance of shipping lanes, inaccessible to unfriendly warships and yet close enough to New Orleans for the sale of illegal merchandise. Jean, the older brother, intelligent, cool and resourceful, was the organizing genius of the enterprise who led the Barataria pirates to fame and fortune.

The city authorities of New Orleans were so afraid of Jean Lafitte's power and influence that they did almost nothing to bring him to justice. The truth was that many high-ranking officials owed their private wealth to the Lafittes, and that piracy and smuggling brought prosperity to the town. The brothers were in fact respected citizens who dressed in expensive clothes, wined and dined in the most fashionable cafés and thumbed their noses at authority. Once when the city fathers plucked up enough courage to arrest them, they hired the cleverest lawyers in town for their defence, and walked jauntily out of the courtroom as free men.

The price of patriotism

On a September morning in 1814 Jean Lafitte received an unexpected visitor, the captain of a brig flying the colours of the British Royal Navy, which had dropped anchor at the entrance to Barataria Bay.

For the past two years, Great Britain and the United States had been at war. Infuriated by trade restrictions and infringement of her neutral shipping rights during the long struggle between Britain and Napoleonic France, the young American Republic saw the war as part of a continuing fight for survival. But although fierce land and sea battles had secured the northern frontiers American forces were hard-pressed from the west and south. British forces had already landed at Pensacola in Florida and their next target was the vital port of New Orleans. Aware of Jean Lafitte's fighting reputation, and bearing in mind that he was French by birth, the British delegation that now requested a meeting with him hoped to persuade him to turn against his adopted country.

The proposition, outlined in a written message from the commander of the British forces in Florida, was tempting. In return for the services of his privateering fleet and crews, Jean Lafitte would receive a commission in the Royal Navy and a personal payment of $30,000. 'Think it over very carefully,' advised the British officer who was handling the negotiations. 'Remember that Louisiana does not rightfully belong to the United States and that there are many people here, British, Spanish and French, who would welcome our victory. Your brother Pierre is at this moment behind prison bars in New Orleans and you and your men are not exactly popular with the authorities. When we liberate the city you will all be free to do what you please. But you must give us an immediate answer. What do you say?'

Jean Lafitte needed time to think it over.

'Not so fast,' he chuckled. 'Gentlemen, I am flattered by your proposition but I have to discuss it with my captains. So you will have to be patient. I will give you my reply within two weeks.'

In fact he had already decided to turn down the British offer. He might have done some unlawful things in his life but he was no traitor. After consulting his colleagues he sat down and wrote a letter to a leading member of Louisiana's legislative council.

'Sir, I am sure you will be interested to learn that I have been approached by the British invading forces...' After outlining the enemy offer Lafitte announced that he was ready to demonstrate his patriotism by placing the services of the privateers of Barataria at the disposal of the U.S. government. He asked for his offer to be conveyed to Governor Claiborne of Louisiana and urged a quick reply.

That very night Pierre Lafitte escaped from prison. The news helped the New Orleans defence committee to come to a decision.

'Form an alliance with those bandits? Never! Our answer will be given personally. The base at Barataria must be attacked and destroyed without delay!'

The news of an imminent American raid on Barataria came as a stunning blow to Jean Lafitte. But although several of his hot-headed captains urged him to resist the punitive expedition Lafitte declared that in no circumstanced would he take up arms against his own countrymen. 'We must agree to whatever they propose,' he said gravely, 'for only then will they be

Jean Lafitte invited to turn traitor

convinced that we are sincere.'

When the American ships entered Barataria Bay they found Jean and Pierre Lafitte gone, together with most of their men. A few dozen pirates, hoping for clemency, were captured without putting up resistance. The abandoned ships of the Barataria pirate fleet were towed back to New Orleans and huge stocks of contraband goods seized. The cannons of Grande Terre and Grande Île were dismantled, the wooden huts along the beaches set on fire. As the expedition sailed away a great column of black smoke rose above the sandy bay of Barataria to mark the end of the Lafittes' pirate empire.

Yet when a British attack on New Orleans was expected at any moment the American military command changed its tune. With only four companies of regular troops and half a

dozen inadequately armed ships General Andrew Jackson was reluctantly persuaded to accept Jean Lafitte's offer. Overnight the men of Barataria became respectable; and, because of their experience in handling heavy artillery they were given the vital task of manning the cannons which formed the main line of defence between the British army that had landed in force at the mouth of the Mississippi and the city of New Orleans. Thanks to the accurate firing of the ex-pirates of Barataria, two attacks by the troops of General Sir Edward Pakenham were beaten back with heavy losses. Then on New Year's Day, 1815 the British took advantage of thick fog to launch a final assault on the American lines. After a sharp artillery duel and bitter infantry clashes the fog cleared to reveal the battlefield strewn with the corpses of red-uniformed British soldiers. They

Surcouf's men board the Kent

had lost more than two thousand men in dead and wounded. At a cost of some sixty casualties the United States had won the battle of New Orleans.

The reward for the gunners of Jean Lafitte who had fought so gallantly was shamefully meagre. Just a personal letter of thanks from General Jackson and a free pardon for the men of Barataria. Despite repeated pleas for justice the U.S. government remained silent. Bitterly disillusioned, Jean Lafitte reassembled his companions and went back to a life of privateering and piracy.

For some years the Lafittes operated from a new base on a sandy island off Texas. But the United States Navy was regularly patrolling these waters and in 1821 the pirates' Texas headquarters were destroyed. Lafitte bowed to the inevitable, and disbanded his crew.

Nine years later he reappeared under a new name as a rich and successful merchant in the city of Galveston. He married, raised a family and lived happily until 1854. His retirement from piracy had coincided with an all-out attempt by the U.S. Navy to clear the Caribbean and South Atlantic for ever of pirates and privateers. When Jean Lafitte died those exciting and colourful days were a distant memory.

Robert Surcouf: last of the corsairs

By an odd coincidence Robert Surcouf, known as the 'king of corsairs', was born exactly one hundred years after René Duguay-Trouin, in the same port of St Malo. But it was not only a birthplace that the two men shared. Both wasted their school-days, misbehaving so outrageously that their parents despaired of their future; both were trained briefly, and unsuccessfully, for the clergy; and both felt the call of the sea so strongly that by their late teens they were already embarked on the only career which attracted them, that of a corsair.

Robert Surcouf served his country as bravely and honourably during the Napoleonic Wars as his famous predecessor did in the War of the Spanish Succession a century earlier. Once again the principal enemy – and, by now, France's only rival sea power in Europe – was Great Britain.

Surcouf's hunting ground was the Indian Ocean and his main bases were the two islands, then both held by France, which are today known as Mauritius and Réunion. After a brief excursion into slave-trading he turned corsair, capturing several merchantmen of the East India Company. For these daring actions Surcouf received praise but little profit, certainly not enough to impress the wealthy father of Marie-Catherine Blaize, the girl he had set his heart on marrying. The twenty-one-year-old Surcouf stormed out of the Blaize house, shouting that he would one day return as a rich man to marry Marie-Catherine.

On August 7, 1800 the look-out man of the *Confiance*, Surcouf's flagship sighted a large English ship in the Bay of Bengal. She was the *Kent*, belonging to the East India Company, armed with thirty-eight cannon and about three times the size of the *Confiance*. Surcouf told his men that they were in for a stiff fight but that when they boarded the enemy he would let each man loose for an hour to take as much loot as he could find. Although the *Confiance* came under heavy fire Surcouf cleverly manoeuvred her close in and soon his men were aboard. In bitter hand-to-hand fighting the French sailors slowly pressed the British back; and when Captain Rivington of the *Kent* was shot dead by an able seaman who had stormed his way onto the bridge, resistance quickly ended. Soon the French tricolour was fluttering at the masthead.

The *Kent* was carrying hundreds of passengers who had been rescued after their ship had caught fire off the coast of Brazil and Surcouf's men, remembering their captain's promise, were soon rampaging through the *Kent*, plundering at pistol-point. As the screams of terrified passengers echoed from below, Surcouf rushed down with his officers to restore order. A corsair he might be but he was no bloodthirsty robber and murderer. When he later set them free, handing them over to an Indian ship bound for Calcutta, they still retained their personal possessions.

Nevertheless it was as a rich man that he returned next year to St Malo to marry his sweetheart. And although French naval power received a shattering blow at Trafalgar in 1805 Surcouf continued to raid shipping in the Indian Ocean – a pirate in British eyes, a hero to his own countrymen. But with the defeat of Napoleon and the end of land and sea warfare in Europe, the glorious days of the French corsairs also came to a close.

The restoration of peace in Europe heralded the decline of privateering and piracy. At the Congress of Vienna in 1815 the nations involved in the recent wars met to rearrange the map of Europe. For ninety years, in spite of local conflicts, there were to be no major naval encounters between the great seagoing powers. When, in the early years of the twentieth century, the world's nations once more clashed in the North Sea, the Atlantic and the Pacific, conditions had changed out of all recognition. Battleships, cruisers and submarines had replaced sloops, brigs and schooners; and the stakes were no longer cargoes of gold but capital ships and men's lives.

The pirate bases in the Caribbean and the Indian Ocean had been dismantled many years previously. In an age of aggressive empire-building, men of adventurous spirit now joined the army or the navy. From time to time a group of self-proclaimed pirates would defy the forces of law and order to bring off a daring, isolated raid on the high seas; but their careers were short. The age of the great pirates and buccaneers was over, the glory and the shame of those dramatic decades buried, but not forgotten, among blue lagoons, swaying palms and sunlit sands.

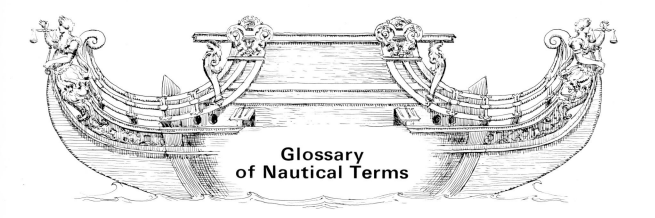

Glossary
of Nautical Terms

Bark. A small sailing ship with three or more masts. Also *barque*.

Boatswain. A ship's officer in charge of sails, rigging, anchors and other equipment. (*Normally pronounced 'Bosun'*).

Bow. The front or forward end of a ship.

Bridge. A raised platform on a ship for the captain or officer in command.

Brig. A two-masted, square-rigged sailing ship.

Broadside. The simultaneous firing of all the guns on one side of a warship.

Cabin boy. A boy employed to look after a ship's officers and passengers, often carrying out other simple shipboard duties.

Caravel. A small three-masted, lateen-rigged ship, especially used in sixteenth-century Spain and Portugal.

Careen. To clean or repair a ship by turning it over on its side.

Carrack. A merchant vessel, sometimes fitted out for war; a galleon.

Convoy. A group of armed escort vessels; a group of merchant ships protected by escort vessels

Cross-staff. A navigational instrument used for measuring the height of the sun or a star.

Cutlass. A short sword with a slightly curved blade, formerly used by sailors.

Deck. A platform running from side to side of a ship, serving as a floor and covering the space below.

Dinghy. A small rowing boat, often towed behind, or carried on board a larger ship.

Dugout. A canoe made by hollowing out a tree trunk.

East Indiaman. A large, armed sailing ship used for trading with the East Indies.

Fireship. A vessel filled with explosives and burnable materials, set adrift to destroy enemy shipping.

Flagship. A ship carrying the flag of the chief officer of a fleet.

Flotilla. A small fleet; a fleet of small ships.

Forecastle. The forward part of a ship; formerly a raised, castle-like deck from which fire could be directed down on an enemy ship. [Also, *fo'c'sle*].

Frigate. A light, speedy sailing vessel, sometimes armed for battle.

Galleon. A large, armed sailing ship, used by the Spaniards and other seafaring nations.

Galley. A large seagoing vessel, propelled by oars and sails, chiefly used in the Mediterranean.

Grappling hook. A hooked device, attached to the end of a rope, used for slinging over a rail or other projection in order to board a ship.

Helmsman. The man at the helm (tiller or wheel) who steers a ship.

Hold. The inside of a ship, below the deck, where cargo is stored.

Hull. The frame or body of a ship, not including masts, sails and rigging.

Lateen-rigged. Having lateen, or triangular-shaped, sails.

Longboat. The largest boat carried by a sailing vessel.

Mainmast. The principal mast in a ship.

Man-of-war. A warship.

Mast. A long pole or spar set upright on the deck or keel of a ship to support the sails.

Masthead. The top of a mast.

Merchantman. A trading ship.

Mizzen mast. The rear mast of a three-masted ship; the third mast of a ship with more than three masts.

Pinnace. A small sailing ship, often used for scouting.

Poop deck. A raised deck, usually with an enclosed cabin, built above the main deck in the stern of a ship.

Port. The left side of a ship, facing forward.

Press-gang. A group of men, commanded by an officer, once employed to 'press' or force other men to serve in the army or navy.

Privateer. An armed ship, or the commander of such a ship, commissioned by a government during wartime, especially to attack enemy merchantmen.

Prize. A ship or property captured at sea, usually in wartime.

Quartermaster. A ship's officer responsible for signals, steering and other special duties.

Rigging. The ropes or chains used for supporting the masts and working the yards and sails.

Rudder. A piece of wood or metal attached vertically to the stern of a boat for steering purposes.

Sailing-master. An officer responsible for navigating a ship.

Sea-chest. A chest or box once used by sailors for storing their clothes and possessions.

Seaworthy. In fit condition to take to sea.

Shallows. An area of water near the coast, not deep enough for a large vessel.

Shoal. A place where water is shallow; a sandbank.

Sloop. A small, one-masted ship; a small warship with guns only on upper deck.

Squadron. A group of warships employed for a special mission.

Square-rigged. Having square, four-sided sails.

Starboard. The right side of a ship, facing forward.

Stern-castle. Formerly a raised, castle-like deck in the stern of a ship.

Stern. The rear end of a ship.